Catholic God, True God

Refuting Arguments Against the
Catholic God From the Modern World

PARKER MANNING

ISBN 978-1-63844-471-8 (paperback)
ISBN 978-1-63844-472-5 (digital)

Christian Faith Publishing
832 Park Avenue
Meadville, PA 16335
www.christianfaithpublishing.com

Printed in the United States of America

To
Ray Fischer

Contents

Introduction: Explaining Intention 7

Who Is God? 9

Addressing the Reality of the Most Famous Old
      Testament Stories..16

Jesus Was God in Flesh..27

A Defense of the Trinity 32

Protestants Severely Misunderstand God 39

Mary, Mother of the Catholic God 63

Biblical Atrocities 67

Bible "Contradictions" 85

A Scientific Argument for God: How Did We Get Here?............92

Analyzing Arguments for God...110

A Closer Look at Objective Morality...116

Concluding Thoughts 125

Notes 127

Introduction
Explaining Intention

Proving the existence of God is the first and most significant aspect of Christianity. One could not possibly argue for anything regarding the Bible without first arguing that God exists. Proving the existence of God will be pivotal, as with that presumption, others can be made. For example, no one can rise from the dead or be born of a virgin, right? This is an argument made constantly by my atheist and agnostic counterparts. However, they are missing key information. If God exists, and He can do all things, He can rise from the dead or have a virgin birth. So first let us prove the existence of God to show that those "impossible things" could happen.

Keep in mind, for the atheist and agnostic reading, if I am unable to show you an objective positive proof of the existence of God, this is not an issue for me. I know I will defend my point quite well. But I do not see an issue with failing to see positive points for God's existence. I see an issue with arguing for negative points of His existence.

For example, there is no positive and undeniable fact that Jesus rose from the dead. For one, I don't see an issue with this. See, the entire point of Christianity is that faith saves us. If there is no faith, there is absolutely no salvation. If the Catholic God exists, He would want us to believe in Him without positive proof. Why this is—I have no idea. I would be lying to you if I told you that I understood every facet of God's existence. Nevertheless, this proof still shows. If you contend that the Christian God helped write the Bible (if He exists), then you cannot write Him off as a nonexistent being because there is no positive proof. As I talked about earlier, this is not only not a problem; it is to be expected.

Before I go into detail over why and how we can know that God exists, I first want to make sure Catholics are aware as to whom they are attempting to spread the Gospel to.

One of the first questions you should ask a potential convert is, "If Catholicism is true, would you become a Catholic?" If they answer "no" to this, be skeptical. After all, a rational person would say yes to this question, regardless of the religion. Islam isn't true, but if it were, I would have no issue becoming a Muslim. If someone says that they would not be Catholic even if they knew it was objectively true, you should not spend much time trying to spread the Gospel to them. To be clear, I am not saying we should restrict the Gospel to anyone. But think about the opportunity costs—if you have two hours to spread the Gospel, why spend the entire time pulling your hair out trying to convert people who, by their own word, would not convert even if they were convinced? Spend a little time on those people, then after a bit, move on to people who are willing to listen.

Now that I have that out of the way, the object of this book is not only that God exists but that Catholics are the only ones who fully understand His will. If that is the case, I fully believe that God desires all to be Catholic. Given that this is true, remember that you should convert if you are convinced. I pray that each and every one of you who reads this book at the very least considers converting to Christ's Church. God bless.

Who Is God?

So who is God? In short, He's an omniscient, omnibenevolent, omnipotent, and omnipresent being. This book will be supporting the idea that He exists. I will not be proving these assumptions now (as I will in the entire book). I am simply going to explain what it means for Christians when they believe those truths.

First things first, however, it's important to talk about what this means. Let's start with the first one. God is omniscient, so He knows everything. Prior to discussing arguments involving God, it's imperative to know that there are some things about Him that the human brain cannot comprehend. We cannot fully comprehend a being that was always here and always will be. Moreover, we cannot understand a being that knows everything in the past, present, and future. He knows what will happen, what could happen, what would happen, and what won't happen.

One important contention before I go on is the argument of who in fact even made God to begin with. This argument doesn't even make sense. The aspect of God is that He is the uncaused cause. I dive deeper into the philosophy of this later in the book. No less, the aspect of God is that He always has and always will be. He does not need a beginning. In fact, if He has one, He is not God. The definition of God is that He is omnipresent. If He is not, He is no longer God. The question quite grossly misunderstands who God is.

Take this for an example: Triangles are shapes with three sides. If you imagine a triangle without three sides, it is no longer a triangle. It is something else completely. This is the same with God. If you take God, remove something that makes Him God, He is no longer God. Therefore, the argument of who made God does not hold up because it throws out a core definition of God, that He is omnipresent.

Going along that line, there are certain things that even I as a religious apologist do not understand about God. For one, I do not understand why God gives people cancer. I also do not understand why God would let a natural disaster kill hundreds, if not thousands. However, this does not negate the existence of God.

Why is this? Well, think of it this way. Let's say God exists. Everyone knows this to be true for whatever reason. If a natural disaster happens afterward, does this mean that God is not all-good and/or all-powerful? This argument only works if you accept that He is not all-knowing (which He is). If He is all-knowing, He would know every possible scenario and use His power to make the best possible scenario happen, Dr. Strange style.

He knows what will happen, what could happen, what would happen, and what won't happen. Meaning, if God is an all-loving and all-good God, then we need to trust what He has in store. These natural disasters do not prove that God is not all-loving. They do, however, show that we do not fully understand His plan. It's also worth noting that it is entirely possible that God will end someone's life before they are able to turn away from Him. God can see this alternate reality. It may be the case that God does this knowing that if this person were to continue living, they would eventually leave God and go to Hell upon death. In this example, God is saving someone from an eternal damnation by ending their earthly life earlier than usual. This theory is not nullified by God ending the lives of atheists either. God would know if that person will ever turn to God. After all, if God knew that this person would eventually turn to Him, He would let them survive longer so that they will come to Him and be saved from damnation. Atheists dying premature deaths at the hands of something like cancer suggest that this person would not turn to God at any point in their life. It's worth noting that some Christians, including myself, believe in different levels of Hell. God can mercifully make an atheist die a premature death if He knows that he will end up in a worse level of Hell if he keeps living.

Why then, should we ask this being for things? After all, if He has a plan, then asking Him for things would not constitute a subsequent change. If you ask Him for something that is already a part of the plan, then there is no need for change. If you ask Him for something that is not a part of the plan, then there will not be a change.

This argument sounds rather compelling. Yet this analogy is much too simplified for something like God. Firstly, God, the concept of God (at least the Christian God), is a being that is outside of time. God can will that something happens in time because of His will outside of time. What I mean by this is that God can ensure or prevent something from happening outside of time given that someone supplicates it inside of time. Outside of time, He knows that you will ask for this specific thing and makes accommodations according to the request. God cannot change His mind, but He can will that something happens outside of time because you asked for it inside of time.

If that sounds implausible, you're not alone. Many do not understand this basic principle of God. To make it easier, consider this analogy: A father has his son's phone. He knows (for whatever reason) that his son will ask for his phone back. However, he is not going to do so until he asks. So when the boy asks for his phone back, and the father gives it to him, this does not mean that the boy asking was pointless. It could be that the father would have given the phone back regardless, but this could have been at any point in time. The son asking for it almost certainly expedited the exchange if it was going to happen. After all, there is an alternate reality where the son does not ask for it back at all. Put simply, just because the father knows that his son will ask for the phone back does not diminish the son's request. This is the same with God. Being outside of time, He knows what people will ask inside of time. He knows what will happen in the past, the present, and the future. So He knows outside of time that people will ask for something inside of time and makes accommodations in that way.

But what is the evidence that prayer actually works? Before we get to that, we need to talk about the answers to prayer given to us by God. If God does not answer a prayer the way we want it to, it does not mean He is not listening or that He doesn't exist. It could just mean that He does not see your request as something that would better mankind. Take a look back at the phone argument in the previous paragraph. If the boy asks but does not get the phone back, does this mean that the father is not listening? Of course not! It just means that the father believes that the son would be better off if he were punished for longer. This is a bad example because it implies that the father in this scenario *thinks* the son would be better off without the phone. With God, He knows the best possible outcome. Nevertheless, it gets a picture in the brain of how God operates.

With that being said, there are three answers that God will give to a prayer. For the sake of argument, let's think about a prayer with which I would ask God for something. Most atheists only view this type of prayer as pointless because of the reasoning above. Their argument, again, was debunked earlier.

The three answers God gives to a request prayer are as follows:

I.   Yes.
II.   Not yet.
III.   I have something better in mind.

Keep in mind that these sorts of things cannot be studied in any way, shape, or form for a couple of reasons. Let's say that we do a double-blind study for prayer. We have a control group with an illness that does not receive prayer. The other group receives prayer. If the results of the experiment do not show that those who received prayers did better than those who do not receive prayers, does this show that prayer does not work? The answer would be no, and there are a couple of reasons for that.

I)   Even if the group didn't do better, this does not mean that prayer doesn't work. After all, God could have the "I have something better in mind" answer for those people.

II)   The Bible says throughout that testing the Lord God is unworthy. It's worth noting that this is in Deuteronomy and not just the New Testament. This is important because it implies that members of the

three great religions all believe that testing God is
immoral. Putting this study up would literally be a
test, throwing out the results of the experiment

The results of prayer are simply anecdotal and will always be.
Prayer cannot be studied. However, we do certainly have anecdotal
evidence that suggests prayer works. A recent example would be
when two parents prayed to Fulton Sheen in an effort to save their
lifeless baby. After over an hour of no vital signs, the baby returned
to normal.[1] Read that again. Over an hour of *no* vital signs, the baby
returned to normal. This baby was dead for over an hour but was
brought back to life. The doctors thought they had lost hope and
were about to call a time for death when the baby began to show
signs of life. This is not clear-cut evidence that prayer works but certainly shows that you cannot argue that it doesn't.

One of the most famous arguments for the existence of the
Christian God would be the argument of morality. This argument
suggests that objective moral values came from a moral compass
(God); therefore, God is real. This argument is certainly rather persuasive. Furthermore, anyone who has studied history for more than
three minutes knows that we have gotten more moral over time. If
morality is subjective, then we did not become more moral throughout the years. We have simply changed our view of subjective morality.

However, I generally do not subscribe to this way of arguing.
Trying to prove God from objective morality is particularly more
difficult than proving an objective moral standard from an omnibenevolent being. People have subjective moral standards throughout
the world that do not line up with God's objective moral standard.
Because when I say, "Murder is intrinsically wrong" to a group of
pro-choice people, they do not care. They either do not believe it to
be truly murder or they don't see it as an intrinsic evil. Be that as it
may, saying "God says this isn't okay" won't persuade those who do
not believe in God. Instead, we should attempt to prove the existence of God then the existence of an objective moral standard. In
doing so, you can equitably prove that being pro-choice is an innate
obscenity.

However accurate it may be, citing God as the objective moral standard has its issues. People look at the actions that people do in the name of religion and see religion as a bad thing. Firstly, although people do horrible things in the name of religion, that doesn't refute the existence of God. This just proves that free will exists. Second, just because people do immoral things in the name of religion does not mean religion is destructive. To say that would be to ignore all the good and moral things that have come from religion. Moreover, saying "all religions are bad" because people did bad things with it is like saying that all religions are good because people have done good things with it. Judging the morality of religions involves getting specific with those religions. Regardless, this does not diminish the existence of God. Citing the number of religions as proof that God does not exist also doesn't make much sense. I'll discuss this in further detail later in the book, but all this does is prove that free will exists. Because God loves us, He allowed us to choose whether to follow Him or not. The world consisting of multiple religions proves this. Moreover, just because you have people doing obscene things in the name of religion does not mean that religion has a net evil. Yes, people have done evil things in the name of religion. But without religion, would we have more deaths or less death? We don't know this obviously. But it's worth noting that many people are moral because of their religion.

The next truth is that God is all-powerful. An argument by atheists would be that if God exists, why is there evil in the world? After all, if God is all-loving and all-powerful, He would have the love and power to stop all war and violence. However, this argument by Sam Harris and other atheist apologetics falls flat because it flies in the face of one of the pinnacles of Christianity; that is, free will. I will be going into much greater detail later in the book. For now, know that God does not force His will onto others. If He loves us truly, which He does, He cannot possibly force us to do anything. That would be the will of an unloving dictator. Keep in mind, the abstract of free will does not mean that we always have complete control over our decisions. However, overall, we do have the ability to choose. I have complete control over whether I go to Mass on Sunday. The only thing stopp_ng me is temptation and my ability to choose (given that there is not something stopping me that is out of my control, such as a blizzard of some sort).

However, even if I were to prove that God exists, it would be an entirely different argument to say that the God of the Bible is the true God. Moreover, it would be even more difficult to argue that the God from the Bible is the same one that Catholics love and worship today. With that being said, you will see a plethora of evidence for that assumption in the forthcoming chapters.

Addressing the Reality of the Most Famous Old Testament Stories

Before arguing the existence of God, I want to first argue that if God exists, He is the God of the Bible. By proving He is the God of the Bible, we can prove He is not the God of the religious books of other religions. By proving that the Old Testament is historically accurate, we can attest that the stories written within the Old Testament could have been inspired by God Himself. If the Old Testament stories are inaccurate, we can throw out the entire Bible (or at the very least, the Old Testament). Because after all, if God inspired the Old Testament, there would be no errors. If there are errors, either God made a mistake or God allowed the people writing it to have an errancy. I will not be trying to prove that every single Old Testament story is historically accurate because this book would be several thousand pages long; rather, I will be looking at the evidence of the more well-known biblical stories. I will also focus on those that are argued by Christians to have actually happened and not symbolic. Proving that the Old Testament stories are historically accurate would prove that the Old Testament is not only historically accurate but that the true God could have been involved in these stories.

Let's start with the most famous Old Testament story: Adam and Eve and the garden of Eden. The first and most obvious question everyone asks first is where the garden is even located. Well, we don't know. The thing about the garden of Eden is that Adam and Eve had everything they wanted. They didn't have to economize like we have to today. They didn't have to worry about predators or go out and find food. They had everything. No such place exists today.

This does not mean the place never existed. It could have existed, then it became null and void after the fall. There's also a possibility someone manufactured over the original garden. We don't know, but we wouldn't expect to find much evidence of a garden that has no problems at all in today's age. In fact, most Christians would not phase at the lack of evidence for the garden of Eden for a simple reason: the flood would have wiped it out. Therefore, it is much more important that I make evidence for the flood than the garden itself since if I am not able to provide evidence for either, Christianity would be nullified.

Let's now look at the evidence for the flood. The flood is not just found in Genesis. Accounts for the flood are also found in the Sumerian King List, Atrahasis Epic, and Eridu Genesis.[2] There are some inconsistencies across the stories. Nevertheless, it shows that there were certainly stories of a large flood at the time.

Opponents of Christianity will say that the Mesopotamian creation myth is eerily similar to the one that Christians claim is true. Even if this were true, it does not mean that the flood never happened. This way of thinking goes the same for all religious thought. Just because a similar event was said to have happened before the next event does not mean the future event is fantasy. In short, just because A and B are similar, and A came before B, does not mean B copied A. And it certainly does not mean that both A and B are fiction if A is determined fictional. The two flood stories do have their similarities, which are as follows: In both stories, there is a flood sent as a punishment; one man built an "ark" (you will see why I put that word in quotation marks later); that man took family and living creatures and survived.

Although these stories have certain similarities, the differences are overwhelming. In fact, Assyrians generally do not see the Genesis flood and the Mesopotamian flood as similar events because of the vast differences.[3]

The differences are so plentiful that it would be egregious as to conclude either having been copied directly from the other. In fact, there are eight large differences:

I. The Mesopotamian gods sent the flood because humans were "too noisy" whereas God sent it for moral reasons (humans needed to be punished for sin).

II. The Mesopotamian gods hid their plan from all humanity (the man who found out was told surreptitiously). In Genesis, God commands a man to build the boat.

III. Noah's ark was built like an ark whereas the Mesopotamian "ark" was a cube shape.

IV. There is no Mesopotamian account or timing of the abatement of the flood.

V. A much larger group of people board the Mesopotamian cube. Noah takes aboard family only.

VI. The details of sending out birds differ greatly between the two stories.

VII. The Mesopotamian builder left the ark by his own merit then did a sacrifice to ask the gods for forgiveness. The story says that the gods were mad at him for surviving the flood. Noah left after God told him to, and his first sacrifice was one of thanksgiving. In Genesis, God wanted humans to continue to survive. In the Mesopotamian story, the gods no longer wanted humans to flourish. This is a major difference in storytelling. In one story, the humans aren't doing anything wrong, but the gods want to destroy them and are angry when one survives. In Genesis, God sees His people doing wrong but does not punish those who are not doing wrong in an effort to continue the human race.

VIII. After the flood, the land in Mesopotamia was replenished by the gods in some measure; but in Genesis, it is left to Noah, family, and the surviving creatures to replenish the earth via natural means.

Now that I have proven that one story was not copied from another, it is still up to me to prove that my story has evidence. Before I do that, I need to discuss what exactly I am trying to prove. Yes, I will argue that the flood happened. But did it happen *exactly* as the Bible puts it? In the New Testament, Peter refers to the flood as such: "For this they willfully forget: that by the word of God the Heavens were of old, and the earth standing out of water and in the water, by which the world that then existed perished, being flooded with water."[4] The Bible refers to the flood as something that happened to the earth (not just a portion of the earth). In Genesis 7:17, the writer also says that it rained constantly for forty days. Certainly, this could have happened. However, I am not a Bible literalist. I also do not see an issue with someone believing there was a massive flood several thousand years ago but that that flood did not exactly happen the way the Bible describes.

This not an anti-Christian idea to take the Bible in a figurative sense. In fact, in other parts of the Bible, it's common sense to take it figuratively. For instance, in Matthew 18:9, St. Matthew tells us to "pluck out our eye" if it causes us to sin. Most people do not view this as him telling us to literally pluck out our eyes but to remove things from our lives that cause us to sin (pornographic magazines would be a good example).

Tradition says that Moses wrote the Pentateuch. The biblical reasoning for this would be Exodus 17:14: "Then the LORD said to Moses, 'Write this on a scroll as something to be remembered and make sure that Joshua hears it, because I will completely blot out the name of Amalek from under Heaven.'" There is still a reliance on tradition if you are going to say that Moses wrote the *entire* Pentateuch and not just Exodus and possibly another. Even that verse does not say Moses was instructed to write all five books. It says that God told him to write something specific within one of the books.

The argument that Moses wrote the whole Pentateuch makes sense until we get to Deuteronomy. Deuteronomy 34:5 recalls Moses's death. This would be a rather unusual thing for Moses to write before his birth, especially in the past tense. I am not ruling out this possibility, however. After all, God certainly could have told

Moses what to write, including his future death, before his future death. It is possible but rather unlikely. To me, there are a few possible answers to the question "Who wrote the first five books of the Bible?"

I.   Moses wrote the entire Pentateuch, even recalling his future death in the past tense.

II.   Moses wrote some of the Pentateuch. Some was written at a later date by another inspired writer(s).

III.   The writer(s) of the Pentateuch is unknown but inspired by God.

The last scenario is not out of question as there are several books in the Bible whose author we do not know, but we still view them as inspired. The last two scenarios are the ones that seem the most likely to me. The first scenario would mean that Moses recalls his own death in the past tense (Deuteronomy 34:5) and calls himself a "very humble man" (Numbers 12:3). Needless to say, people who pride themselves on being humble are not usually humble in all actuality. That isn't to say that Moses didn't write any of the Pentateuch. He may have written the first part, and someone else (this could have been more than one person) wrote other parts.

If Moses didn't write the entire Pentateuch, this could possibly mean that the events that happened didn't happen *exactly* as described. Now, of course this is not to say the Bible is in error in any way. The purpose of this chapter is to prove that the Old Testament has no errors. But even so, if the Pentateuch is a recollection of stories passed down by people via word of mouth, it could have happened in a slightly different way than transcribed in the Bible. (Keep in mind, before I get into the realism of the Pentateuch, that this isn't an issue for Catholicism. You do not have to believe that the events in the Bible happened exactly as transcribed. You simply must believe that the Bible is the true Word of God and that the vital parts of the stories happened; i.e., that the exodus happened, that Adam and Eve existed, and so on and so forth.)

Even so, if Moses wrote Genesis, who's to say that God could not have allowed Him to write in a figurative way? I talk about this verse more in a later chapter, but in Exodus 32:14, Moses essentially says that God changed His mind and decides to not punish a certain group of people.

Now obviously God cannot change His mind. The only way that a being would change his or her mind would be if presented with new information that contradicts the information already at hand. Of course, this doesn't work if the being whose mind you are trying to change knows *literally* everything. If Moses wrote Exodus, did God allow him to write fiction? Of course not. Rather, it made it easier for people to understand what was happening. God did not change His mind. Rather, He knew outside of time He would not punish those because He knew Moses would ask Him not to the inside of time.

With that being said, just because a flood happened that was not exactly forty days, or covered the *entire* earth, does not mean that the Pentateuch was not inspired by God.

But where is the proof that this sort of thing happened? Let's think about the ark. Had this happened, there would be no way to find the ark itself. Wood decays and breaks apart, which would make it extremely hard to find thousands of years later. We would not expect evidence of the ark outside of the Bible. (Keep in mind, just because we cannot physically see the ark does not mean it didn't exist. Lack of evidence does not constitute negative evidence.)

I will be more focusing on the idea that there was a massive flood. One theory that has gained a lot of traction is that when the Mediterranean and Aegean waters fell into the Black Sea (fresh water at the time), it became known as the great flood. Not only that, but in 1996, two marine biologists from Columbia State University, Dr. William B. F. Ryan and Dr. Walter C. Pitman, claim that this happened around 5600 BC[5] (yes, around the same time Noah would have been alive). This seems to be the most well-known theory, even years later. This would likely be the flood unless we find new evidence in the future that contradicts that claim. I could go into detail about other theories, but that is not the focus of the book. (For more on this, check out William Ryan and Walter Pitman's book: *Noah's Flood: The New Scientific Discoveries about the Event That Changed History.*) Needless to say, there is overwhelming evidence that a great flood happened.

Keep in mind that we would not expect to find overwhelming evidence that these people existed. Records at the time were clearly not as well-kept as they were several thousand years later. If I am not able to overwhelmingly prove that these specific individuals existed, it does not mean they didn't exist. It simply means that our historical account of people at the time is not as clear-cut as it could be.

This argument makes sense until you start talking about the exodus. Why would a culture as well-documented as the Egyptians make no mention of the Israelites, slaves, a plague, or any of the other things the Bible claims to have happened? As you will see, this contention holds little ground. We do not have any Egyptian records that specifically mention the Israelites, Moses, or a massive exodus involving this group. We have no *explicit* traces of Israelites. But how well do these oppositions hold up?

We would also not expect to see a lot of evidence of the Israelites from the side of the Egyptians. If we are looking at the Bible's account of the exodus, the pharaoh seems extremely stubborn and unwilling to accept defeat. (I talk about this much more in my "Biblical Atrocities" chapter.) Nevertheless, if the Israelites existed and escaped from Egypt, would we expect to see Egypt to be proud of this? Of course not! So why would we expect them to have hieroglyphics of their defeat? We shouldn't assume that they would. Yes, the Egyptians were meticulous record keepers. But they would not meticulously record their defeat. Keep in mind, I am not attempting to make an argument for either side here. I am simply saying that the lack of proof for my side is not positive proof for the other.

Okay, so maybe we wouldn't expect to see Egyptian writings of the defeat and the exodus thereafter. But if the Israelites were in Egypt for so long, why don't we have proof that they were even there? We know the Egyptians kept many records. But how many were lost? After all, things can get lost and destroyed after thousands of years. As stated earlier, the Egyptians most likely would not have plastered their defeat all over the place. But why don't we have any positive proof that the Hebrews were enslaved in Egypt at all?

Even though we have many artifacts from ancient Egypt, we will never have the vast majority of the papyri. Around 99 percent of New Kingdom papyri are lost forever.[6]

That being said, there are still several positive proofs of the biblical exodus. These include, but are not limited to:

I.   Israel and neighbors Edom and Moab are mentioned in firsthand Egyptian sources shortly before 1200.

II.   The Ramesside Nineteenth Dynasty abounded in Egyptian society at all levels, from Pharaoh's court down to slaves.

III.   The Bible's account of the exodus reflects real places, not imaginary ones. There had to be an understanding of the land to write it. For instance, salt-tolerant reeds, water from the rock, habits of quails, and other things show that the author needed to have a great understanding of the area. These narratives are in contrast with other stories written at about the same time.

IV.   The restriction on going by a north route to Canaan is a direct response to the Egyptian military presence there in the thirteenth century.

V.   There is Egyptian technology involved in the tabernacle (an ancient Semitic concept). How could they have Egyptian technology, or even know of it, if they were never there?

VI.   The Merneptah stone mentions the Habiru people. Some view this as a general term for those in the area as it is used both ways in the Bible. However, the troops must have identified themselves as Israelites for him to use that language. Otherwise, they would have called themselves Judeans or Ephraimites or whatever else. At the very least, the Merneptah stone corroborates the existence of the Hebrew people in Egypt at the time.

VII.   The form and content of the Sinai covenant fit only the late second millennium.

VIII.   The apparent gap of six hundred years between the origin of Deuteronomy and its possible seventh-century role is certainly not out of the ordinary. (Not to mention, biblical texts exist during that gap.)

IX.   The main features of Deuteronomy go back to at least the second millennium.[7]

While the exodus cannot be proven objectively, it wouldn't make sense for it to be. Even so, we can make an inference that it *probably* happened because of context clues. Many atheists believe Deuteronomy was written at a much later date. Even if that is true, how would the author(s) have such an admirable understanding awareness of the area? These events have not proven to have happened, but knowledge of the time period would put the exodus in the "Much more likely than not to have happened" category of historical events.

Ancient records also indicate that an assortment of Asian peoples settled in the East Delta. According to cuneiform documents, among these people were known as Apiru (also called Habiru and Hapiru). Many scholars believe this refers to the nomads in the East Delta region. Nevertheless, the Hebrews, as depicted in the Bible, would certainly fit within that parameter.

Even if there are no written records, we should still have DNA and skeletons from these events, right? In actuality, it would be rather unusual for these to have been kept intact. Even the most well-preserved Egyptian bodies (mummies) do not have DNA attached to them. Stephan Schiffels, leader of the Population Genetics Group at the Max Planck Institute for the Science of Human History, had this to say about it:

> "Researchers were generally skeptical about DNA preservation in Egyptian mummies, due to the hot climate, the high humidity levels in tombs and some of the chemicals used during mummi-

fication, which are all factors that make it hard for DNA to survive for such a long time.[8]"

So if the most well-preserved Egyptians cannot keep their DNA, why should we expect a Hebrew slave to have DNA tracings?

Another contention is that we should at least have evidence of things the Israelites brought with them on the exodus, even if we can't determine DNA. Well, for one, the Israelites would have used tents or some other temporary measure for housing. They certainly would not have built permanent housing. After all, would you build a permanent house knowing you would be moving again very soon?

Even if we contest that the exodus happened, why did it take so long for the Israelites to get to Canaan? The Bible says it took forty years, but it would only take a few days to walk that distance today. So what gives? Well, here are some things to consider:

I.   The Israelites were moving a massive group of people. The more people, the slower you travel. Just ask big families how vacation goes.

II.   As depicted in the Bible, the Israelites went to war on more than one occasion. Obviously, that would slow them down as well.

III.   The Israelites would not have gotten to Canaan in three days without the help of God. It would stand to reason that either

    i.   God doesn't exist and the Israelites just decided to settle in Canaan. This possibility is overwhelmingly unlikely, considering what has happened before. For the Israelites to do this massive exodus without God is rather preposterous.

    ii. Or more likely, the Israelites did not want God's help wandered as a result.

I could go on forever about the historicity of the Old Testament, but I wanted to cover the most well-known contentions in this book. For more information, check out K. A. Kitchen's *On the Reliability of the Old Testament.* Kitchen goes into great detail explaining the historicity of the text, much more so than I intend to do here. Nevertheless, the idea that the Old Testament is just fabricated stories deprived from who-knows-where was overwhelmingly disproven throughout this chapter.

Jesus Was God in Flesh

Many debate who Jesus was. Christians believe that He was God. Other monotheistic religions, however, believe that Jesus was merely a prophet sent by God and not God Himself. If this reality is in any way accurate, Christianity is completely disavowed. Luckily for my Christian brothers and sisters, this is wholly inaccurate. We have several historical accounts that prove that Jesus not only rose from the dead but ten of the twelve Apostles were martyred because they refused to admit that He did not.[9]

Why would these men die horrible deaths to assist in a lie? There would be no reason to do this. Some were crucified, some were stoned, one was even dragged around the city until his body was in shambles. No one is insane enough to do this for a lie, let alone ten people closest to Jesus who did so.

If Jesus rose from the dead, then there would be no argument on whether He was God. If non-Christians could prove that Jesus never rose from the dead, Christianity would be wholly denied. As St. Paul says in his first letter to the Corinthians, "And if Christ has not been raised, your faith is futile; you are still in your sins."[10] Dismantling the idea that Jesus rose from the dead ruins any other Christian philosophy. However, the compelling argument is on the side of Christians. This is because those opposed cannot possibly spin this philosophy any other way.

Those opposed to Jesus being the Son of God have several counterarguments. Most philosophers agree that Jesus existed and died.[11] The idea that Jesus not only existed, but died on from crucifixion, is hardly debated among secular scholars. It is so scarcely argued that I am not going to even touch on it in this chapter. Rather, I am going to focus on the supposed aftermath: the Resurrection. Many debate, however, whether He rose from the dead. Firstly, if he died, the body would have to be somewhere. If he didn't rise from the dead, we should know where the body is.[12] Why don't we know where Jesus's body is?

There are several types of scenarios that could have happened to the body. Firstly, someone could have stolen the body. However, there would be no incentive for anyone to steal the body. The Romans wouldn't have because they would have wanted the Christian people to keep quiet. Had Jesus's body been missing, Christians would have been completely despondent. They'd shout things about Jesus having been risen and that He truly was God (that which they did). If the Romans had had the body, they would have given it up to decrease commotion among the Christians and Romans.

However, what if the Jews stole the body of Jesus? These leaders also would have no motive to steal the body. A risen Jesus would only stir up Christianity, which is the opposite of what Jews wanted. They killed Jesus to shut Him up along with His disciples. After all, if He were truly God, He would have stopped the abuse. When Christians started saying that Jesus rose from the dead, Jews would have given up the body to prove Christians wrong. If this would have happened, Christianity would have stopped then and there.

Another theory suggests that Christians stole the body. This theory makes the most sense out of all the "stolen body" theories. After all, it would have been easy for Christians to say that Jesus rose from the dead if His body was not there. However, this theory makes little sense because of the Apostles' gruesome deaths. It would be immensely illogical for them to steal the body, then die horrible deaths claiming they saw Him alive. Furthermore, it would be nearly impossible to actually get the body from the tomb for several reasons. So if the body wasn't stolen, there must be another reason it wasn't in the tomb.

Some insist that the Apostles were hallucinating. However, there is no way that all ten of them were hallucinating the same thing at the same time; this isn't how psychology works. Several things can cause hallucinations, but groups of ten people do not see the same hallucination. Even if they were all hallucinating the same thing, that still doesn't answer the question of where Jesus's body was during all interactions.

Another theory suggests that the woman who first said the body was missing went to the wrong tomb. However, this makes little sense. If this were historically accurate, Roman soldiers would have shown the body of Jesus to those who believed He rose from the dead to stop Christianity. Again, the Roman soldiers killed Jesus to diminish Christianity. If the body was still in the tomb, they would have made it present to stop Christianity from spreading. Moreover, the woman would have known that this was the wrong tomb because the tomb where Jesus was born was well-known at the time.

So what if Jesus never died? This theory also makes little sense. The medical data goes against it heavily; His wounds, the crown of thorns, and the time spent on the cross would all go against this theory. If He never died, His recovery in three days would have been impossible from today's standard of medicine, let alone two thousand years ago.[13] Not to mention, centurions made sure Jesus was dead.[14] Mistakes were not allowed. If Jesus never died, there would be severe consequences for the centurion. All other theories don't make sense. If they were willing to die for their faith, the disciples would have seen Jesus. Therefore, Jesus rose from the dead.[15]

Even if you were to make the argument that we should have more evidence of Jesus's resurrection, this does not nullify the evidence we have. As I have shown, we have a multitude of evidence that Jesus not only existed but rose from the dead. Of course, we could always have more. Couldn't we have more evidence that, let's say, Alexander the Great existed? "Well of course we could have *more* evidence, but we have enough to conclude that He existed." Why then can we not constitute the same thought pattern for Jesus? We have overwhelming evidence that He not only existed but rose from the dead. Just because we could potentially have more evidence should not abrogate the evidence presented. If we are to argue that a man not only existed but rose from the dead, we need to have evidence for such claims. But saying "Why isn't there more?" would only work if there is insufficient evidence of His existence (as shown with the

Alexander the Great example). As shown earlier, this evidence is still extraordinary even with the argument for the lack thereof.

This is especially important in regard to the previous chapter. As I have already proven, Jesus not only walked on earth but was God in flesh. As God, when He references Old Testament figures, it would stand to reason that they existed. Since Jesus discusses Old Testament figures several times, there are only a few possibilities.

I. Jesus existed and said these things but was not God.
  i. His statements wouldn't hold much ground.
  ii. Proven incorrect by the beginning of the chapter.
II. Jesus didn't exist.
  i. I have shown this to not be the case.
III. Jesus existed but may or may not have said these things.
  i. It would be extremely hard to historically prove *everything* Jesus said was historically accurate. What would be easier would be proving that the writers of the Gospels knew Jesus (again, this was proven earlier in the chapter), then that the writers of the Gospels died for Jesus. Proving those two things would be extremely easy and already done countless times. As a result of these two realities, we should trust what these people had to say about Jesus. After all, what is the alternative? They lied? Highly unlikely (again, considering they died for Jesus, they would not have made Him up or fabricated things He has said).
  ii. In order to say that Jesus is not God, you would have to say prove that the martyrs who died saying He rose were either lying or did not die for that reason. You would also have to explain why the tomb was empty and where the body went (and is now). Finally, you would have to say that the writers of the Gospels were lying or that the supposed writers of the Gospels did not actu-

ally write the Gospels. This would be quite the challenge.

Objection 1: People die for beliefs they have all the time. Why is it an argument for Christianity that the Apostles were martyrs but not an argument for Islam when that individual dies for his beliefs?

Reply to Objection 1: The argument is not that the Apostles died because they *believed* Jesus rose from the dead. The argument is that they died because they said they saw Jesus, two completely different scenarios. Why would they lie about that? They know whether or not they saw Jesus, it is not a matter of faith. Meanwhile for the Muslim, it is all a matter of faith in Islam.

I've shown throughout this chapter He not only died but rose from the dead. Only God would be able to do such a thing. Therefore, Jesus was God. This is one of the main reasons why I'm writing this book. Christians everywhere need to be reminded that their faith is strong and truly one of God. With this presumption, it can be assumed that Christianity is the true religion.

A Defense of the Trinity

As I have already proven, the Bible is the inspired Word of God. But how should we recognize God in this book? The Trinity is the most vital part of Christianity, but also it is one of the most confusing. How can God be three persons but one being? This is something that Christians have been pondering over for centuries. How can God be three separate persons but one singular God? But, just because humans cannot fully understand it does not mean it is inaccurate. While the word "trinity" is not in the Bible, it's clearly referenced. When you say, "I had a cup of joe," it means you had coffee. Just because you didn't say the word "coffee" does not mean it was not very clear what you were talking about.

The trinitarian philosophy revolves around the idea that there are three persons in one God: Father, Son, and Holy Spirit, not three separate gods. To be Christian, one must believe in the Trinity and that Jesus was God, not just a prophet. As I will argue further, the Trinity is a biblical doctrine, even if it is not fully comprehended by humans.

First things first, when thinking of "the Father, the Son, and the Holy Spirit," one should use singular verbs and antecedents. Jesus used a singular object of the preposition in Matthew 28:19 when He said, "Baptize then in the *name* of the Father, Son, and Holy Spirit." When we think of three persons, we think of three people, with three distinct names. For example, Jason, Steve, Jessica are in a room. You would not say, "The name of the persons in the room is Jason, Steve, and Jessica." The person hearing that would think you are just learning English. This is not the same with God. You could say, "The name of the persons of the Trinity is the Father, the Son, and the Holy Ghost," and it would be grammatically correct even if it sounds unusual. There are three persons but one God. Therefore, only one name.

Each person is God, but each person is not the other person. Meaning, the Father is not the Son, is not the Holy Spirit, is not the Father. There are not three Gods. Moreover, there are not three forms that God comes to us in, a heresy called modalism.[16] There are three separate persons but one being (God).

Each person has a divine nature. The Father has a divine nature, the Son has a divine nature, and the Holy Spirit has a divine nature. However, the Son also has another nature, the human nature. Jesus Christ is both fully God and fully man. He is not some half-God, half-human creature. He is completely both, with two wills.

A common argument against comes from people that do not understand how Jesus can be fully God and fully man. After all, if He is God, He cannot be man, right? This means that there are certain things that God cannot do. This would undermine who God is if this were the case. But it is not. God becoming a man does not undermine His omnipotence. Islamic apologists will claim that Jesus Christ cannot be God because God cannot become man. This philosophy comes with the idea that if God becomes man, He is weakened and is not fully God anymore. Therefore, God cannot become man. But as I have argued already, this is not the case. God is not weakened, but He has two natures in Christ instead of just one (like in the other two persons).

In fact, saying "God cannot do this" is not a route I would recommend going down for those who believe in Him (unless you're talking about Him overdoing His own power, which is something I discuss in a later chapter.).

Jesus Christ can do anything as God but cannot do anything as man. He has two natures and two wills. Can He explain string theory? As God, yes, He can. As a human, no, He couldn't. That scientific philosophy was not prophesized yet, so Jesus as a man would not know what that is. But He is also God, so how does He not know everything that has ever happened or will happen? Well, He does, but not as a human. This is extremely difficult to understand, make no mistake. But saying "I do not fully comprehend God's existence, therefore He cannot exist" is a rather doltish argument. After all, our brains literally cannot comprehend the concept of infinity.

We think of everything as contingent. People are born then die. They are here for a short period then die. This is what has happened with every organism for millennia. For example, imagine if Michael Jackson was never born. No, not that he never existed. But that he was always here and always will be here. Michael Jackson was since the beginning of time. But he was here before that. After all, if he was always here, he was here an infinite amount of "time" before time existed. He was always here. This is such an out-there way of thinking that human beings cannot possibly fully comprehend it. Obviously, Michael Jackson has not been here forever. He was born and died. This was merely an example to show that our brains cannot fully comprehend who God is. We do not fully understand God, but that does not mean He does not exist. Moreover, it does not mean that if we do not understand something He does (i.e., becoming fully man while keeping His divine nature) that He cannot do it.

I used the string theory example a couple of paragraphs ago. There are biblical examples of this as well. In Matthew 24:36–37, Jesus says, "But about that day or hour no one knows, not even the angels in Heaven, nor the Son, but only the Father. As it was in the days of Noah, so it will be at the coming of the Son of Man." Does this mean that Jesus is not God because He says He does not know when He will be back? Surely not! It means that His human nature does not know, but His divine nature does. The Father and the Son are distinct, but He is one God. If that's confusing, you can read it as "While He was on Earth, Jesus's complete omniscience was 'veiled' and that is why He did not know at the time." He didn't know at the time because it was hidden by God the Father, but He knows now that He is in Heaven. He is still God, but because He is fully man, He cannot know certain things as a human. Remember, He is fully God *and* fully man. Jesus's divine nature has existed forever, but His human nature came into existence around the year 0.

We know this from several Bible verses. The first, and most well-known, is John 1:1: "In the beginning was the Word, and the Word was with God, and the Word was God." Who is "the Word" that John is referring to here? "The Word" is Jesus Christ. How do we know this? Well, later in that same chapter, John says, "And the Word became flesh and dwelt among us, and we have seen his glory, glory as of the only Son from the Father, full of grace and truth."[17] The Word (God) became flesh and dwelt among us. Jesus Christ is God. He has always been God and always will be God, but He became man and dwelt among us. Then later, in John 10:30, Jesus says, "I and the Father are one." He is one God, not two or three. There are three persons in one singular God.

There are a few verses that "nontrinitarian Christians" (an oxymoron, by the way) will use to cite their heretic beliefs. As I stated earlier, the word "trinity" is not in the Bible, but that does not mean it is not referenced. Anyway, Mormons, Jehovah's Witnesses, and other nontrinitarians will cite 1 Peter 3:22 as evidence that the Son and the Father are not equal, but the Father is more impactful than the Son. Peter writes, "[Jesus] has gone into Heaven and is at God's right hand-with angels, authorities and powers in submission to him." This philosophy suggests that since Jesus is at the "right hand" of God the Father, He is less than Him.

This does not mean that Jesus is not God and does not mean that He is less important than the Father. In fact, in our creeds, the Church claims that Jesus is now "seated at the right hand of the Father." Another verse they will cite is Acts 2:32. Luke writes, "God has raised this Jesus to life, and we are all witnesses of it." Using the same thinking pattern as before, is Luke saying that Jesus is less important than God the Father? Of course not! God (Father, Son, and Holy Spirit) raised Jesus (fully God and fully man) from the dead. In fact, we know that this is what Luke meant because Paul makes it clear in his first letter to the Corinthians. "By His power God raised the Lord from the dead, and He will raise us also."[18] We have only one God, so Paul uses the article "the" in this sentence. If Jesus Christ were just another God, like the Mormons and Jehovah's Witnesses say, Paul wouldn't have used an article at all. He would've just said, "God raised Jesus from the dead." God's divine nature raised Jesus's human nature from the dead. God's divine nature raised Jesus's human nature from the dead and allowed Him to prophesize after

His death here on earth. Later in that same verse, it says that Paul and the Corinthians will be raised as well. It would be rational to assume that this applies to everyone and not just Paul and the Corinthians. This is not an argument for universalism. Paul is just saying that God will raise us to Heaven if we continue in His presence. This does not mean we will all rise from the dead like zombies. But it does mean that death is not permanent. Rather, death is a change in location.

"But Paul also says that the head of Christ is God in that very same letter![19] Surely, this must mean that God the Father is better than God the Son!" In a way, this is true. God the Father is the head of God the Son's human nature. Just like God the Son's divine nature is the head of the Son's human nature. No human is the head of God. That is all Paul is saying here. (This same thought process can be applied to John 14:28 when Jesus says that the Father is greater than Him.)

Knowing this, every other verse that nontrinitarians will use are thrown out the window. When Jesus says in Matthew 28:18 that all authority has been given to Him, it does not mean that God the Father's divine nature is more important than God the Son's divine nature. It means that God the Father's divine nature is more important than God the Son's human nature. Similarly, Jesus's divine nature is more important than His human nature. God needs to give authority to a human on earth. Authority over Christianity comes from God. Authority does not come from humans unless those humans got their authority from God (apostolic succession).

Nevertheless, the last verse I want to address is John 17:3–5. This argument seems to make sense from the nontrinitarian side but is quickly refuted by reading further. Jesus says, "Now this is eternal life: that they know you, the only true God, and Jesus Christ, whom you have sent. I have brought you glory on Earth by finishing the work you gave me to do. And now, Father, glorify me in your presence with the glory I had with you before the world began."

Nontrinitarians will just look at John 17:3 and say, "The Father sent the Son, so the Father is more important!" As I have already shown, this argument doesn't hold up. Not to mention, if you continue reading, Jesus says that He had glory with God before the world began. Jesus Christ's divine nature existed at for all time, but His human nature was created by God.

Easily the most overlooked person of the Trinity is the Holy Spirit. Is the Holy Spirit truly a person or just a force? After all, a dove cannot do things that a person can do, right? Well, the Bible suggests otherwise. In the Gospel of John, Jesus says, "But the advocate, the Holy Spirit, whom the Father will send in my name, will teach you all things and will remind you of everything I have said to you."[20] If the Holy Spirit is able to teach people things, then He is a person and not merely a force. In the book of Acts, Luke writes, "The Spirit told Philip, 'Go to that chariot and stay near it.'"[21] If the Holy Spirit can do things like teach and speak, then He is not just a force. Forces cannot do these things. The force of gravity did not teach me how to read. It would be right to assume that the Holy Spirit is a person and not just a force.

I think it's also vitally important that I clear up some misconceptions about the Trinity by refuting heresies that have been condemned by the church. While there is no perfect illustration for the Trinity, the following analogies do us all a disfavor because they usually make people misunderstand what the Trinity truly is.

I.   Partialism is the idea that each person is one-third of God. This analogy sometimes comes from St. Patrick's example that the Trinity is like a three-leaf clover (although, that certainly wasn't what he was attempting to do). Each person is not a third of God. Rather, each person is God with a singular God being.

II.   Modalism is the idea that God is not three separate persons but three forms of God. This heresy is often attributed to the idea that God is like water in that it has three forms (solid, liquid, gas). This heresy is believed most notably by Oneness Pentecostals. Those who believe this ideology run into major problems during the baptism of Jesus, the times when Jesus talks to the Father and when Jesus says He will return to the Father.[22]

III.   Finally, the *filioque* is something that sets Catholics apart from Orthodox folk, but the Catholics are the ones who are correct here. Before answering why Catholics added "and the Son" to the Nicene Creed, we first must know that the Church did not change her teachings. Yes, the original creed just said that the Holy Spirit proceeds from the Father. However, adding "and the Son" is only a contradiction if the original teaching was that the Holy Spirit proceeds from the Father exclusively. The Bible also reaffirms the Catholic position on the *filioque*, as Jesus says in John's Gospel that He will send the Holy Spirit.[23] Lastly, in the book of Revelation, John says that an angel showed him the river of the water of life, flowing from the throne of God (the Father) and of the Lamb (the Son).[24] This is a clear callback to John's Gospel where he refers to the Holy Spirit as "rivers of flowing water."[25]

Although the Trinity is a confusing concept, it is a biblical one. To deny the Trinity is to deny that God can do all things or that Jesus is God. Both statements do not hold up. Proving the Trinitarian philosophy is a pivotal point in arguing that the Catholic God is the true God since that is a major philosophy for Christian theologians.

Protestants Severely Misunderstand God

You may be wondering to yourself, "Why didn't you name the book *Christian God, True God?*" That would be a hard definition because there's too much ambiguity on who the Christian God is. There are certainly parts of God that are not debated among Christians. For example, we all believe that God is all-knowing, all-good, and all-powerful.

Some of the biggest and most egregious misunderstandings of God come from people who claim to be Christians. I have already proved that "nontrinitarian Christian" is an oxymoron, and these people who claim to be Christian do not understand God. The typical definition of *Christianity* goes like this: "a monotheistic, Abrahamic religion based off the teachings of Jesus Christ." The last portion is what I want to tackle in this chapter. If a group claims to be Christian but does not abide by the teachings of Christ, their God does not exist, and their religion is null and void of purpose.

Because even if someone were to say that they hold to the teachings of Christ, do they? Imagine if someone said that they believe that Jesus Christ is the Son of God and that He was born of a virgin, died on the cross, and rose from the dead. But then they say that Jesus was a unicorn who slayed dragons. Is this just a "misunderstanding of the same Jesus"? Or is it a complete and total removal of who Jesus was? Clearly, it's the latter. I understand that no one believes that Jesus slayed dragons. But the analogy still applies to other milder scenarios of people who misunderstand Jesus. If your church is not based on the teachings of Jesus Christ, then you are not a Christian. Because of this, we need to know who the God of the Bible is.

Regarding core Protestant doctrines, it's important to note that no one taught them in the early church. No one taught that scripture is the sole infallible authority, and no one taught faith alone. If you don't believe me, I would encourage you to find one who believed these things. Keep in mind that this is not the same as believing that Scripture is a final authority, or that we do nothing to earn salvation. Church Fathers did teach this, and this is something the Church teaches as well. In order to meet this challenge, you must show me a Church Father who believed that scripture is the sole infallible authority for Christians (Sola Scriptura), and one who believed we are justified by God by faith alone (Sola Fide). If Protestants are not able to find one (as I am sure they will not), they will have to admit that they believe that *all* of the early Christians were wrong on these key Protestant doctrines. I do have to give Protestants credit for this as it takes an enormous amount of pride to look at the entirety of Christian history and go, "They are all wrong. Every single one of them."

Even Protestant historians admit that justification by faith alone was not taught anywhere before Luther. For instance, Protestant author Alister McGrath admits in his book on the history of the Christian doctrine of justification that sola fide was a "theological novum."

"A fundamental discontinuity was introduced into the western theological tradition where none had ever existed, or ever been contemplated before. The Reformation understanding of the nature of justification as opposed to its mode—must therefore be regarded as a *genuine theological novum.*"[26]

Notable anti-Catholic church historian Peter Schaff also admits in his book about church history that those looking for the Protestant doctrine of justification by faith alone in the church fathers will be "greatly disappointed."

"The doctrine of the *subjective* appropriation of salvation, including faith, justification, and sanctification, was as yet far less perfectly formed than the objective dogmas, and in the nature of the case, must follow the latter. If anyone expects to find in this period, or in any of the church fathers, Augustine himself not excepted, the

Protestant doctrine of justification by faith *alone*, as the 'articulus stantis aut cadentis ecclesiae' he will be greatly disappointed."[27]

Rejecting this unanimous consensus raises two main problems for Protestants that will be addressed further in the chapter. First, it introduces the idea of a Great Apostasy. The Great Apostasy is the idea that the Gospel was completely lost for a period of time. Protestants claim to reject this, as it's contradicted by Scripture (1 Timothy 3:15, Matthew 16:18–19). However, if they are going to make claims such as Luther did that Sola Fide is "the doctrine by which the Church stands and falls" and no one taught it until Luther, we would have to say the church fell until Luther.

It doesn't just end there. There's not only unanimous consensus against the reformed view of sola fide, or sola scriptura. There's also unanimous consensus that Baptism saves, one can lose salvation, priests can forgive sins, the Deuterocanon is inspired Scripture, intercessory prayer to saints is valid and prayers for the dead are efficacious. Don't believe me? Try to find one person who rejects any of these things before the year about 400. In fact, the great majority of these things were not rejected until the reformers came along and fabricated their version of the Gospel.

I want to go back and explain how persuasive of a point this is for me. Jesus taught His Apostles; His Apostles taught their successors (or whomever you want to call them). Their successors taught their successors, and so on. We call this the Covenant Community. This community is one of the reasons we can conclude that Jesus was God, or at least claimed to be since they all said that He was. Whatever this community unanimously attests to, we should hold to. Two reasons:

I.   It just makes logical sense. How could Jesus and the Apostles teach something that gets wrong unanimously immediately thereafter? How does that even happen? For instance, lets take Baptismal Regeneration (the idea that Baptism actually saves and is not a sign and symbol of one's salvation). This idea is unanimously attested to in the early church, no one denied it. I would encourage the readers who disagree to give me anyone who did, but I will also give a scholarly source for my assertation. J.N.D. Kelly, an Anglican scholar, in his book *Early Christian Doctrines* wrote, "From the beginning baptism was the universally accepted rite of admission to the Church…as regards to its significance, it was always held to convey the remission of sins."[28]

FURTHER QUESTIONS:

Why did the Apostles choose these guys to be their successors if they did not care about their teachings? Was this community influenced by someone? Did they just not read Scripture? Why did God allow for the message to be lost so quickly? These questions and more can be raised. Needless to say, it's an untenable position.

II.   This is one of the reasons we know the four Gospels are Scripture. If we can use that reasoning to get to the four Gospels, it is rational to use that line of reasoning for other things that are also unanimous. (I develop this idea further in a couple of pages)

Objection 1: Jesus clearly teaches eternal security in Scripture, so it does not matter what the early church said

Reply to Objection 1: I want to run a thought experiment for the objector here to show them that if their point is correct, it proves too much. Consider a scenario in which Jesus teaches eternal security of the believer:

Premise 1)   Jesus teaches eternal security
Premise 2)   Eternal security is part of the Gospel
Premise 3)   He also said the gates of Hell would not prevail

Premise 4) No Christian until Calvin taught eternal security, so no one knew the true Gospel until Calvin

Premise 5) Because no one knew the Gospel until Calvin, one would have to say the gates of Hell prevailed until Calvin

Conclusion 1: Even if Jesus taught eternal security in Scripture, we should not listen to him at all, since he clearly contradicted himself

Conclusion 2: Since Jesus contradicted Himself, He cannot He God. As a result, Christianity is thrown out the window

An insistent objector will most likely object to Premise 4. They will say that while eternal security is a part of the Gospel, if someone does not believe in eternal security, they can still be saved.

This objection works until we use a similar argument for Sola Fide. If justification by Faith Alone is "the Gospel" (as many Protestants have argued) then this line of reasoning works with that substitute, since no one taught the reformed view of Sola Fide until Luther. Furthermore, if Luther is correct when he says that Faith Alone is "the article by which the church stands and falls.[29] We would have to see church fathers teaching justification by faith alone in the patristics Since we don't (at least, not the Protestant version of faith alone) we would have to conclude that the Gospel was lost for 1500 years.

Because of this line of reasoning, even if I believed something was taught in Scripture, I could not believe it if it was unanimously rejected in the patristic era.

Knowing these facts about Church history, a question I like to ask Protestants is, "Given that the Great Apostasy is not true, what should the early church look like?" We know that the Great Apostasy cannot be true because if the gates of Hades prevailed against the Church for a period of time, then Jesus was incorrect when He told Peter in Matthew 16:18 that the gates of Hell would *never* prevail. This is an excellent question to ask because the early Church certainly doesn't look the way. If Protestantism is true, the Great Apostasy had to have happened. If the five Solas are the Gospel, we should expect to see this taught everywhere in the early church. Since Sola Fide and Sola Scriptura are not taught in the early church, Protestants are forced into believing in the Great Apostasy. Even if I were to grant to a Protestant for sake of argument that Polycarp and Clement taught Faith Alone, the Protestant would only be left with a Great Apostasy that happened slightly later in time. Because, after this, Christian writers wrote overwhelmingly about praying for the dead and confessing sins to a Priest to be forgiven, and if they believe those things, they cannot logically hold to the reformed view of Sola Fide.

Secondly, in his book, "What is Reformed Theology?" Protestant apologist R.C. Sproul argues (in a chapter defending sola fide) that "If we reject the truth claims of the Gospel, we cannot be justified" and "The reformers believed that in condemning justification by faith alone, the Roman communion was in fact condemning the biblical Gospel itself." In order to be consistent, Sproul would have to say that no one was saved before Luther, and that the Gospel was lost for 1500 years (unless he believes someone can be saved while condemning the Gospel itself, which would be unusual to say the least).[30]

Some will argue that the church was just "underground" as some independent fundamentalist Baptists believer. However, to illustrate how ridiculous this belief is, let me give an example:

> "Do you believe Alexander the Great was a fire-breathing dragon? No? This was the reality. We have writings that say he was a human, but that's just because those who denied the truth killed those who tried to spread it."

The trail of blood theory is simply some fringe conspiracy theory that anyone could use. "No, Joseph Smith did not make up these doctrines. The writings were just destroyed." Furthermore, consider how implausible it is that *all* of the writings in the early church of the "true Christians" were destroyed.

This brings me to my next argument regarding Protestant beliefs in the early church. This was an argument that became known to me by Michael Lofton, a Catholic Apologist. I will be taking a slightly different approach than Michael does, but nevertheless, wanted to credit him anyway. The argument goes like this: "How do we know that the four Gospels are Scripture and not the gnostic texts?"

There is actually a correct answer to this. It is not subjective. We know that Matthew, Mark, Luke, and John are inspired Scripture because the Covenant Community (the people who knew the Apostles along with the people who knew the people who knew the Apostles) that was entrusted the revelation from the Apostles unanimously said that these books were Scripture. "We can trust their unanimous opinion", the Protestant tells me. But, unfortunately, for our Protestant here, if we are to logically follow this line of reasoning, one would have to throw out Protestantism as a whole. If we are going to say that because the Covenant Community held a unanimous belief on x, we can trust that x was handed on from Jesus to the Apostles to the Covenant Community, we would have to trust that things like Apostolic Succession and that one can lose salvation are both true, among a plethora of other things that Protestants deny.

I would also argue that if it is logical to use the argument that the first followers of Jesus all said He was God, therefore we can attest that He made that claim, it is logical to use that line of reasoning to reject things like eternal security. Think about it—if it's logical to say to a Muslim, "The first followers of Jesus all said He claimed to be God, so we can reasonably assume He claimed to be." Then in order to be consistent, we would also say it's reasonable to believe things like eternal security are wrong because the first followers of Jesus all rejected it. Not only would a Protestant not be able to use this argument, but they would have to show why the hypothetical argument I gave to the Muslim fails. If that argument is valid, Protestantism as a whole is refuted. If it is acceptable for a Protestant to deny one thing that this community unanimously accepted, why would it be wrong for someone to say that the four Gospels are not Scripture?

Furthermore, Protestants absolutely reek with pride when they argue that the people who were taught by someone who was taught by an Apostle were unanimously wrong but the Church they started last weekend in the building of an old Chuck E. Cheese has the Gospel completely correct.

Lastly, for my reader, think about how quickly Christianity spread in the beginning stages. Now, think about how unlikely it would be that something was unanimously taught by all of the Churches that was not taught by the Apostles. Using this line of thinking, one cannot possibly be Protestant and be following the Gospel. This point is made further when one recalls that formal sufficiency (something Protestants hold to) requires that the "important" things in Scripture are clear. Since their version of Sola Fide is not taught anywhere in the patristics, they would have to conclude that either that issue is not important or no one read Scripture until Luther.

I will now be going through seven objections that I'm sure you will run across if you bring forward these arguments to Protestants:

Objection 1: Even if intercessory prayer is unanimously attested to, I don't like praying to Mary, so I don't do it
Reply to Objection 1: Using a similar logic flow, one could say that they don't like the four Gospels, so they aren't going to view them as Scripture.

Objection 2: While things like Baptismal Regeneration were unanimous in the early church, the Church Fathers were all wrong because that view contradicts Scripture
Reply to Objection 2: Putting aside the fact that this Protestant believes that the Church Fathers unanimously believed something that they believe is so plainly contradicted by Scripture, they also undermine their ability to use said Scriptures if they are going to use them against the Covenant Community to whom the Scriptures were entrusted. When this community unanimously says the Gospel of John is Scripture and also unanimously says that in John 3:5 Jesus says we have to be Baptized to enter

Heaven, it would be ridiculous for us to listen to one statement and not the other. Why can we just pick and choose?

Objection 3: Several Church Fathers say we are justified by Faith Alone

Reply to Objection 3: Yes, however, they are not using it the way the reformers used it. Since these guys all believed in prayers for the dead being efficacious (we know this because many write about it, and no one writes against it), they cannot possibly believe in Sola Fide the way the reformers put it.

Objection 4: Paul rebuked Peter. This just goes to show people can get stuff wrong and it doesn't pose a problem for Christianity.

Reply to Objection 4: This is just one person. It's a completely different thing to say everyone before the 1500s is completely wrong. Furthermore, this objection undermines the point because Paul corrected Peter. If Protestants are right, everyone before Luther was wrong about key issues and no one corrected them.

Objection 5: Things like eternal security are not actually unanimously rejected in the early church.

Reply to Objection 5: We can determine what is unanimously taught by looking at a lack of schisms based on these issues. For instance, in a debate with Trent Horn over eternal security, James White made the claim that Fulgentius, a saint and church father living in the 5th and 6th century, believed in eternal security. He did not provide a quote, so I cannot look at any specific saying. However, say James was correct. Wouldn't Fulgentius and his church break off and call the other churches heretics for not believing in eternal security? Wouldn't a council have been called on the matter, especially since we know other churches did not teach eternal security? This did not happen, so we can logically assume that Fulgentius did not teach eternal security.[31]

Objection 6: Why should we care about what these fathers teach? I only care about the Bible

Reply to Objection 6: Among other reasons stated above, this objection doesn't work because the consensus of the fathers is the reason we know the New Testament consists of 27 books. How can we trust their 27 book New Testament if they got the Old Testament, Baptism, Justification, and a plethora of other very important things wrong? How can we trust the early church's particular articulation of the Trinity (three persons in one God, co-eternal and co-equal) when those terms aren't in Scripture, yet we can't trust basically anything else they said? If these guys are a bunch of heretics who believe in Baptismal Regeneration, Confession of sins to a Priest praying to Saints, and so on, how can we trust their 27 book NT and their articulation of the Trinity? It simply doesn't make sense.

Objection 7: There are other reasons we know the 27 book New Testament is true other than this consensus

Reply to Objection 7: I have yet to see any other acceptable reason. Even so, even if there was another reason to accept the 27 book New Testament canon, if one uses the consensus of the Fathers as a one of her reasons, she would have to be consistent and say the consensus of the Fathers can be used to advocate for things like the Deuterocanon as well.

All in all, there are four main reasons why we should care about the unanimous consensus of the Fathers.

I. It just makes logical sense. Imagine for a second Jesus teaches what you believe about Baptism, then the Apostles tell their successors the same thing. Then what happens with the successors? Because they unanimously believe what I believe. Did they just not read Scripture? Were they influenced by someone? Why did the Apostles choose these people if they didn't take them seriously? It just doesn't make sense

II.   You undermine your ability to use Scripture if you are going to use it against the covenant community who gave the Scriptures to you. Think about it, the only reason we know which books are the 4 Gospels is because of this community. There are two reasons this matters. Firstly, we are using something unanimous (let's say the Gospel of John) to reject something else that was unanimous. But if we are doing that, we undermine our ability to use the Scripture in the first place! Secondly, how can we trust them to get the NT if they got everything else wrong, including the OT?

III.   Believing that the Gospel was lost concludes Great Apostasy. Matthew 16:18, 1 Timothy 3:15 among others refute this.

IV.   It's extremely prideful to say that everyone before me is wrong because I cannot possibly be wrong.

The question is not "is this Protestant belief logical?" Rather, it is "is this belief so persuasive that we can reject all of Church history?"

Another problem this gives Protestants is in regard to their belief that Scripture is formally sufficient (Sola Scriptura). Protestants constantly say they care about tradition, that Sola Scriptura is not anti-tradition, and so on. They will say that making Scripture the only infallible source of faith does not mean that they do not care about tradition. It is not "Me and my bible under a tree" as James White famously notes. They may say this. However, Protestantism rejects several unanimous traditions of the Christian church, as I have noted. This means that Protestants claim that they care about tradition while simultaneously rejecting unanimous traditions because they conflict with their personal interpretation of Scripture. So, they do not actually care about tradition, and Sola Scriptura actually is "me and my Bible under a tree".

Given the arguments presented, it is quite obvious that Protestants have absolutely no claim to the early church. But to those of you who still think you do, allow me to ask, "Which church father should I read?" Which one is Orthodox? Let's take away Clement and Polycarp because we only have access to one of each of their writings. Which father should I read? You will not be able to give a sufficient answer, because each father you could cite believes something that Protestants deem as heretical.

Another issue that arises with this is the canon. We have already talked about the four Gospels but let's take a look at the entire New Testament. How can we trust this community's New Testament when they got the Old Testament canon, justification, authority, and other things seriously wrong? It makes no sense. Again, Protestants are being inconsistent.

But now, I must actually refute these doctrines. I've already proven Jesus was God in the previous chapter. Because Jesus was divine and knew everything, He would know that He needed to create a church. Why is that? I explained this in my first book, *Fundamentals of Catholic Theology in Just Over 100 Pages*, but I will reiterate here. There was no Bible when Jesus died. There was an Old Testament, but there certainly wasn't impartiality on which books should have been included. If Jesus does not create a Church, it would be exceptionally hard to know which books belong in Scripture. All we would have is a mix of books, letters, and Gospels, along with some apocryphal books that no one would know were not inspired objectively without a church to tell them.

So this rules out the nondenominational crowd as being the ones who understand God almost without much effort or thought at all. If Jesus truly didn't create a church, then how do we know what the Bible is objectively? Short answer: we don't. Jesus knows everything, so He would have known that for people to best understand Him, they need to know which books to read about His teachings. There is no other way to do this without a church unless they believe Jesus descended from Heaven directly to give us the KJV translation of the Bible.

One of the most offensive mischaracterizations of God comes from some of the Calvinist views of Predestination, that God actively desires some to go to Hell. In Calvinism, salvation is entirely monergistic (God does everything, you can do absolutely nothing). The logical conclusion to this would be that if this is true, the souls in Hell are in Hell because of something God did not do. Even the most Thomistic views of Catholic predestination do not go this far. They would still say that everyone has the potency to be saved. This is a gross misrepresentation of who God is. This is not to be confused with God knowing what is going to happen. This theology suggests that God not only knows what is going to happen but that He wants it to happen. Yes, God is all-merciful. Yes, people are punished accordingly and justly in the afterlife. But God does not want anyone to go to Hell. Nothing good can come out of that.

Something viewed as atrocious from our eyes could turn out good because of something called the ripple effect. What we see is a hurricane that wipes out a town. What we don't see is a future where that town's ancestors wipe out the population because of some sort of war. It sounds ridiculous, but it could certainly happen. Remember, God knows what will happen, what won't happen, but most importantly for this matter, what could happen. Good can come out of something that looks dreadful; we just cannot see the ripple effect it has.

This is not to be confused with someone who goes to Hell. When someone goes to Hell, nothing good comes out of it. What kind of ripple effect could possibly happen after someone goes to Hell? What sort of good happens because someone went to Hell? There is none. You cannot possibly say, "God is loving" and "God wants some people to burn in a fire eternally." These two realities cannot coexist. "Moreover, Paul makes clear in his letter to Titus that the grace of God that has appeared offers salvation to all people."[32] It's also worth noting that the Greek word for *all* could include exceptions. However, this is likely not the case. To clear up confusion, Paul could have easily said all of (His people) or all (the elect). This way of thinking also applies when looking at verses that say God desires "all" to be saved. The authors could have very easily said He desires all (of you) to be saved. (or like the previous example, the elect) to clear up any confusion. Because none of the authors do this, it is being read into the text rather than being taken from it.

Again, let me reiterate. This is not to be confused with God knowing that someone will choose to go to Hell and not Heaven. This theology suggests that God wants some people to go to Hell and not that He only knows what will happen in someone's eternal life. That is the theology I am attacking.

The predestination argument relies on the notion that God is all-powerful, and He can do anything He wants. Following this logic, God would most likely do what He wanted, as an omnipotent being could. If God wanted everyone to go to Heaven, He would allow them all into Heaven. However, just because God created certain people knowing that they'd go to Hell, that does not mean He wished it to happen. God certainly wishes that everyone be saved, but that may not be possible with totally free beings. If we are truly free, then some of us will choose to not go to God.

Something else happening contrary to what God wants does not undermine His omnipotence. It just means He didn't do what He wanted to. He certainly could have saved everyone. But some people do not want to be saved, and He accepts that.

Consider this analogy: Imagine that I am a lifeguard of a shark-infested ocean. I do not want people to go into the ocean, as it's infested with sharks. I also have control over whether they go in. I can press a button that stops people in their tracks before they hit the water. Let's say that people run toward the ocean. If I do not press the button, does it mean I hate those people? Does it mean that I actively wanted those people to get eaten by sharks? No, of course it doesn't. What it means is that I saw that they did not want to be alive. They did not want to be saved by me, so I did not save them. It's not as if I did not want to; it's that they did not want to.

"Why would a loving God send people to an eternal fire in the first place?" an atheist might state. However, this logic does not follow. If I have the choice of either Heaven or Hell, and I do not do things that take me to Heaven, then I have chosen Hell. God did not send me there. Along that line, there are also Christians who refute God's existence through misunderstanding Him. Knowing that someone is going to Hell is not the same as wanting someone to go to Hell. Through their belief in predestination, Calvinists destroy the idea that an all-loving God can exist.

Their main theology revolves around the idea that God "predestines" people to Heaven or Hell, and there isn't anything you can do about it. "God wants certain people to go to Hell," as one of my former Calvinist friends argued. If an all-loving God exists, why would He actively want people to go to Hell? Either God is all-loving or He wants some individuals to burn in an eternal fire. You cannot possibly have it both ways. Moreover, this philosophy is rejected by scripture. In the Second Epistle of Peter, he says, "The Lord is not slow in keeping his promise, as some understand slowness. Instead he is patient with you, not wanting anyone to perish, but everyone to come to repentance."[33]

"God wanted the fall to happen," as I have heard from my Presbyterian counterparts many times. This theology actually makes sense at a surface level. Obviously, if the fall never happens, Jesus never comes. Only God knows what happens in that timeline. But if God not only knew the fall would happen but actively wanted it done, why were Adam and Eve punished? They did what God wanted. Then they were punished after. This seems asinine and doesn't make sense from a logistical parenting perspective.

Think of it this way: Imagine you and your (future) spouse want your kids to do something specific. Let's say, take out the garbage. They then do it. As a result, you punish them. What kind of monster parenting is this?

Now, this obviously isn't the same thing as punishing someone for doing something you specifically told them not to do (i.e., eating fruit from a tree after being told not to). I do not want to straw man the opposing argument. However, the same philosophical train of thought still applies. If God (or a parent) want your kid/creation to do something, it's rather immoral to then punish that being for doing such thing.

"But mankind is totally depraved, and we all deserve Hell, so it isn't immoral for God to elect certain souls to salvation and let the rest suffer their eternal punishment. Calvinists will argue that we are totally (not just mostly) depraved because of Adam's sin. The question then becomes, "Who made Adam sin?" According to John

Calvin himself, it was God who "arranged" Adam to sin. "God not only foresaw the fall of the first man, and in him, the ruin of his posterity but also at his own pleasure arranged it".[34] If Calvinism is true, the souls in Hell are in Hell because God arranged the fall, and then did not do something that would have prevented this eternal punishment from happening.

Because of this, the Calvinist view of God goes like this:

I.   God not only foreknew the fall, he arranged it.

II.   He punished Adam and Eve for the sin that He arranged.

III.   When we are born into this world, we are totally depraved because of Adam's sin that God arranged.

IV.   Because God arranged the fall, He has to elect certain souls to salvation. This means that God creates people who have absolutely no chance of getting to Heaven, and because of their total depravity that God arranged, they will spend eternity in Hell.

Not to mention that if salvation comes entirely from God, and that there is *nothing* humans can do to receive salvation, then there is absolutely no reason to evangelize. The only reason I evangelize is because I want people to come to God. The common response I see Calvinists give to this is, "We evangelize because God commands us to." Okay, but why does He command us to? In your view, evangelization does absolutely nothing. Why would you waste your time trying to get people to come to God if it is entirely God's doing? Not only that, but if God commands us to evangelize, there must be a reason for it. If God is commanding us to do something that has no purpose, He is irrelevant and unworthy of worship. The logical conclusion then is that the Calvinist view that evangelization is completely pointless and irrelevant cannot possibly be true.

There are some other verses that Calvinists will use to promote their faulty ideology. I am not going to go through each one by one.

Rather, give you a few general rules when looking at verses that Calvinists will cite.

- o First, God can choose people knowing they will say yes. God chose Mary to be the mother of Jesus knowing she would say yes. Calvinists take this too far when they say that Mary (and anyone else) had no choice at all. And oppositely, Calvinists believe God punishes those who sin against Him. But if they had no choice in their sin, why would God punish them? God's just nature does not mean people are punished for things they had no control over.
- o Next, all Christians agree that God gives more grace to some than others. We don't know why He does this, but this is not an argument for Calvinism. God giving more grace to person A than person B does not equate to God hating person B or not giving him sufficient grace to be saved. God gives everyone sufficient grace to be saved, but some receive more than others (for instance, someone with same-sex attraction is going to have a harder time being sinless than someone who does not have those attractions).
- o Finally, when authors of scripture say that God "hates" certain people, they most likely are exaggerating. We see this throughout scripture. What is most likely happening is God is not happy with what that person is doing but still loves them unconditionally. The Calvinist idea that God "hates" certain individuals doesn't make sense given His all-loving nature but also doesn't make sense given His all-knowing and all-powerful nature. Why would God create something that He knows He will hate or already hates (or is hating)?

There are a few more Bible verses that Calvinists will use to affirm their false doctrine of double predestination. The first would be John 6:44 where Jesus says, "No one can come to me unless the Father who sent me draws him; and I will raise him up at the last day." This does not mean that everyone drawn by the Father is raised up. There are really two parts of this verse that need to be broken down.

- "No one can come to me unless the Father who sent me draws him." Jesus in this part of the verse seems to be saying that no one can come to Him without the Father giving that individual sufficient grace to come. No Christian disputes this.
- "And I will raise him up on the last day." Jesus is the one that raises us on the last day. It is an insertion to the text to say that Jesus is saying He will raise them (even if they show that they do not want to be with Him in Heaven by their sin). Without adding beliefs into the text, you cannot possibly get unconditional election and perseverance of the saints from this verse.

Not everyone who receives God's grace is going to accept it. If we have to, and it is forced love, then it is not true love. Just before this, Jesus says, "All those the Father gives me will come to me, and whoever comes to me I will never drive away." Does this verse indicate the Calvinist view of unconditional election? Let's look at the original Greek to find out. The Greek translation makes it very hard to make the Calvinist argument here. The Greek words for "all that" translate to *pan ho*. This is immensely important. The gender here is neutral rather than expected masculine. This suggests that John wanted to make clear that Jesus meant the entire church as a whole rather than specific individuals, as John would have used the Greek word *pas* to refer to specific individuals.

Another verse that Calvinist will cite regarding their false predestination philosophy is Romans 8:29–30: "For those God foreknew He also predestined to be conformed to the image of His Son, that He might be the firstborn among many brothers and sisters. And those He predestined, He also called; those He called, He also justified; those He justified, He also glorified."

First, it's worth noting that predestination and free will don't have to contradict. Yes, God has a predestined plan. But that plan coincides with free will. God knows what decisions we are going to make, but that does not mean we are not free. The plan that God set forth when He created the heavens and the earth included human decisions. Knowing this, the rest of the passage is null and void. God foreknew that these people would come to Him willingly, and the predestination included them getting to Heaven because of their free will choice to go to Heaven.

Second, and more importantly, there is a reason that not a single Christian taught the reformed view of this verse. This verse leaves open the possibility that people can be called but not predestined to go to Heaven. Note that someone can be justified and glorified but not go to Heaven. Scripture leaves open this possibility, and this is something the early church taught as well. Justification merely means "to become right with God," and glorification means "to ascribe honor to." God can make us right with Him and ascribe honor to us by dying on the cross for instance, but this does not necessarily mean we will be with Him in Heaven.

Keep in mind that just because God's love does not leave us does not mean we are eternally secure. St. Paul in his letter to the Romans discusses this: "And I am convinced that nothing can ever separate us from God's love. Neither death nor life, neither angels nor demons, neither our fears for today nor our worries about tomorrow—not even the powers of Hell can separate us from God's love. No power in the sky above or in the earth below—indeed, nothing in all creation will ever be able to separate us from the love of God that is revealed in Christ Jesus our Lord."[35] God still loves us even when we sin, but that does not mean we are guaranteed Heaven. God loves us all and if we choose to reject it, we do not lose God's love. God still loves those who do not accept His love.

That means Calvinists do not understand God and who He is. Therefore, the Calvinist God is a myth. But what about the other Protestant religions?

One of the main arguments that differs Protestants and Catholics is the idea of eternal security. This philosophy suggests that once we are saved, we cannot lose that salvation. As I am about to prove, this is a gross misrepresentation of who God is.

The main argument Protestants will contend with is that "once we are in His grasp, we cannot leave Him. If we can do so, we nullify the ability of God to keep us in His possession." This philosophy, they say, is backed up by John 10:28 when Jesus says that no one can snatch them (meaning, people who have eternal life) out of His hand.

However, that verse has nothing to do with eternal security. The proclamation made by Jesus is that there is no outside force that can take us from His grasp. This is not the same thing as deliberately walking away with one's own power. You cannot "snatch" yourself from someone else. This is not how grammar works.

However, take away this Bible verse for a second. Why would a loving God force people to stay with Him? Imagine this tyrannical rule in a country. Your friend is trying to amplify this country. He says, "This country is great. The leader is benevolent. I like the atmosphere of amiableness."

"That sounds great," you exclaim. "Have you been to other surrounding countries?"

"Oh," your friend says. "You cannot physically leave. They do not let you. They say it's out of love."

This scenario that I just described is absurd, to say the least. Even if this country is the best place in the world to be, the leader telling his people that they cannot leave is rather oppressive. God allowing us to leave Him does not diminish His omnipotence. Rather, it means that He loves us so much that He does not force us to love Him.

We even see these sorts of interactions among human beings. For instance, when two people date for an extended period, an attachment gets made. Let's assume their names are Peter and Jamie. If Jamie tells Peter that she doesn't love Him anymore and does not want to be with him, what is the loving, Christian, moral thing for Peter to do? Certainly, "leave her alone" is the only plausible option. If Peter were to force Jamie to continue the relationship (keep in mind, this is different from asking her to politely reconsider), that would not be loving. This is the same thing with God. When we want nothing to do with Him, He lets us leave.

Because of course, He could hypothetically force people to stay with Him. However, He does not do this. This is only something that an oppressive government would do. The tyrannical God from a couple of paragraphs ago is the only God that can exist for these people. Given that that is the case, either their version of God is the real God (the tyrannical one) or God does not exist. Because if God is a tyrant, then the God of the Bible is not the true God.

I am not denying the fact that God wants everyone to be saved. Does Jesus only love certain people? That's not the Jesus I know and love. Regardless, just because God *wants* people to be saved, this does not mean that everyone will be saved. After all, God has a passive will and an active will. His passive will is what happens in regards to salvation. If people are truly free, then some people will choose not to be saved. You cannot have one or the other. If we are free, then some of us will not want to be saved. Because we are free creatures, some of us will not be saved. Saying "God wants everyone to be saved!" does not mean anything, considering all Christians believe this.

Not to mention, if Protestants truly believe that all of their future sins were forgiven when Jesus died on the cross, why even repent? They are already forgiven after all. There is absolutely no need to ask for forgiveness if Jesus already said, "This one's on Me." Jesus's sacrifice on the cross is the most perfect thing I can conceptualize, but it was not an atonement for all sins of the future. People still need to ask for forgiveness and be one with God's grace because sinning shows Him that you do not want to be with Him. People can say whatever they want, but showing Him that they want to be with Him is more important. If they do not want to be with Him, He does not force them.

Some will argue that if someone is truly "with God," they will never leave Him. If this is the case, the hypothetical raises some others. For instance, how can one possibly know if they are with God? If you say that someone's Christianity is importantly based on whether or not they leave God in the future, then no one can say they're a Christian. Do you go to church, pray, read the Bible, among other things? Well, none of that matters (apparently). You still cannot call yourself a Christian because you do not know if you are going to leave Christianity in the future.

This philosophy that those who are with Christ cannot/will not leave Him is asinine, to say the least, and is easily disproven by reading the story of Lucifer. Lucifer was in Heaven, rebelled against God, and is now known as Satan. This one-sentence story dismantles the argument that those who are "truly Christian" will not leave God (the philosophy continues by saying that those who leave God were not truly Christians in the first place). So let me ask: Is/was Satan a Christian? Because if you believe that Christians are just people who believe that Jesus came to earth and died so that sins could be forgiven and people could get to Heaven, then Satan is certainly a Christian. He believes in all of those things. As James says in his book, "You believe that there is one God. Good! Even the demons believe that—and shudder."[36]

There are certain verses that say you have to believe in order to get to Heaven.[37] One says that you must be baptized as well, but Paul tells the Romans very explicitly that God brings salvation to those who believe. This seems to reject the Roman Catholic view pretty clearly on salvation, which is that we must do some sort of action in order to regain salvation. "Clearly, we only have to believe that Jesus Christ is Lord and we are saved," as Protestants have said many times.

But let's think about this for a second. What are we believing? The authors never say that all those who believe that Jesus is Lord are saved; that is something that has been falsely implied for centuries. Even if that's what it means, it should at least go further than that. We also must believe that these stories written about Jesus are true and His Bible to go along with it. This is a huge difference because instead of the verse saying, "Salvation is brought to those who believe Jesus is God" to "Salvation is brought to those who believe the Word of God"—a seemingly small difference with astronomical differences. One says you simply must believe that Jesus was God. Other than that, you can believe anything, i.e., that Jesus wants us to kill Jews and Muslims, that rape is acceptable, among others.

"Obviously, this is ridiculous. Those who advocate for the murder of others are not saved," a Protestant would object. "Aha!" I say. So you admit that this verse is saying that we must believe in the Word of God, in both the written and unwritten form?" This includes the parts of the Bible that command us to have action along with faith. In fact, we know that Paul did not mean to say that we are saved by faith alone because he tells the Romans in 2:6 that God will pay them for what they have *done*.

Even so, some Protestants say you don't have to do anything in order to be saved. You merely have to believe in Jesus. That philosophy is rather ridiculous as Satan and the demons in Hell believe in Jesus. Why are they not in Heaven?

If you just have to believe in God/Jesus to be Christian, and all Christians are guaranteed eternity in Heaven, then Satan must be in Heaven now. This logic obviously doesn't make sense as Satan cannot possibly be in Heaven. Hell was created for him and the rest of the fallen angels. Satan certainly believed in God, so shouldn't that have granted him eternity? If not, then you must admit several things.

I.   Those with God can leave Him by their own will (a throwback to predestination earlier in this chapter).

II.   You are not saved eternally simply because you were saved at one point, Satan was surely saved at one point. He was in Heaven after all.

III.   Not everyone who believes in Jesus' divinity will go to Heaven.

Nevertheless, even if you argue that Satan is not a Christian now because of his action, you still have another task at hand, one that is much larger; that is, was he *ever* a Christian?

Let's go by the general Protestant definition.

I.   Belief that Jesus died for sins of people.

    i.   In his case, this would have happened before Jesus came to earth. However, the analogy would still apply by saying that Lucifer believed it would happen at some point.

    ii. Even if he wasn't aware that Jesus would die on the cross in the future, you couldn't argue that he didn't have God's grace. He was literally with God.

II.   He was doing good deeds as a result of God's grace.
  i. While I cannot prove this, it would seem accurate.
  ii. What else did he do in Heaven? Just sat there?

Most Protestants believe that these are the parameters for being a Christian. I would argue for more, like not believing in heresies like eternal security. Alas, if Lucifer were with God and has more intellect than us humans, he certainly wouldn't believe in those things.

The first proof is pretty undebatable. He was with Jesus, so He certainly would believe in Him. He still believes in Him to this day. The second would only make sense. After all, he is in Heaven. All in all, there are only two possibilities here:

I.   Satan was not a Christian even though He was with Jesus in Heaven.

II.   While Satan was truly a Christian at one point, he left that life for a life of sin. If this is the reality (and it's the one that seems much more conducive), then a genuine Christian can lose salvation.

All in all, because Protestants grossly misrepresent who God is, I could not have possibly named the book *Christian God True God*. There is too much ambiguity there, and what some people view as the "Christian God" is inconsistent with common sense and what we know about the Bible.

Mary, Mother of the Catholic God

One major difference between the Catholic God and the Protestant God is the view on Mary. Many Protestants unfortunately do not hold her to the degree with which she should be held. However, that is not the purpose of this chapter. The purpose of this chapter is to analyze the evidence that Mary appears to people and is not merely a hallucination. I will not be going into the evidence of stories that have been proven wrong or stories that have yet to be judged on. I want to more focus on the apparitions approved by the Catholic Church.

I am going to start with the earliest ones and go further into the future. The earliest instance would be Our Lady of the Pillar. This apparition was supposedly seen by St. James the Apostle in Zaragoza, Spain. The liturgical veneration was approved in 1730 by Pope Clement XII.[38] Tradition holds that St. James the Greater evangelized in Roman Hispania (modern-day Spain). James had great difficulties in his conquest to spread the word of God. In AD 40, while he was praying by the banks of the Ebro at Caesaraugusta (Zaragoza), Mary bilocated from Jerusalem and appeared to James, accompanied by thousands of angels, to console and encourage him to continue his work.

Next in history is Our Lady of Walsingham. In 1061, Richeldis de Faverches claimed that Mary showed her, through a vision, the house in which the Annunciation took place and asked her to build a replica. Around five hundred years later, King Henry VIII's soldiers sacked the priory at Walsingham, killed two monks, and destroyed the shrine. The nearby Slipper Chapel was reestablished by Pope Leo

XIII in 1897. This is the only Marian apparition approved by the Church of England.[39]

Next up on the list is Our Lady of Mount Carmel. According to Carmelite tradition, Mary appeared to St. Simon Stock, a prior general of the order in the thirteenth century. The earliest reference to the tradition of his Marian apparition states that Mary appeared to him holding the brown scapular in her hand, saying, "This is for you and yours a privilege. The one who dies in it will be saved."

In 1490, Mary supposedly appeared to Benedetto Pareto in Monte Figogna, Italy. This apparition is known as Our Lady of the Watch. Pareto reported seeing an apparition of Mary on top of Monte Figogna on August 29, 1490. Pareto claimed that Mary appeared to him and asked him to build a church atop the mountain. Pareto at first refused, but he eventually built a small wooden structure. In time, this gathered many pilgrims and is now contained within the Shrine of Our Lady of the Watch. The shrine was elevated to a minor basilica by Pope Benedict XV in 1915.[40]

Our Lady of Good Health (also known as Our Lady of Velankanni) actually has two apparitions.

The Basilica of Our Lady of Good Health in Velankanni commemorates two distinct but similar apparitions in India. The first was in 1570 and the second one in 1578. In each instance, a local child reported a woman appearing and asking for milk to feed her infant. This one should be met with ultimate skepticism as a child reported the events. However, each appearance was followed by a miracle, leading people to believe that Mary appeared with baby Jesus both times.[41] This shrine was also elevated to a minor basilica in 1962 by Pope John XXIII.

One of the most well-known Marian apparitions is Our Lady of Guadalupe. In 1531 in Mexico City, Mexico, Juan Diego Cuauhtlatoatzin and Juan Bernardino claimed to see an apparition of Mary.

Mary supposedly asked there to be a church built at the place of the apparition. The local bishop did not believe his story. After also appearing to Diego's sick uncle Juan Bernardino, Mary imprinted an image of herself on Diego's cloak. The cloak is on display at the

Basilica of Our Lady of Guadalupe in Mexico City. This apparition was approved and confirmed by the church.[42]

Next in line is Our Lady of the Good Event. This apparition lasted much longer than the other ones, from 1594 to 1634, and took place in Quito, Ecuador. This apparition was supposedly seen Servant of God Mother Mariana de Jesus Torres, 1611.

A religious sister, Mother Mariana de Jesus Torres reported that the Virgin Mary appeared to her at the Conceptionist Convent in Quito, Ecuador. According to Mother Mariana, Mary requested that a statue be made in her likeness. Mary also made several predictions, saying that the church and the world would enter into a period of crisis beginning in the mid-twentieth century, and that this period would be followed by a complete restoration. (This would most likely be the Second World War.) This apparition was approved by the church in 1611 by Bishop Salvado Ribera Alvalos.[43]

Our Lady of Šiluva was an apparition that supposedly took place in Šiluva, Lithuania, and was witnessed by a group of non-Catholics.[44]

Because of the reformation, many people around Šiluva converted to Calvinism. As a result, a Catholic church building in Šiluva was eventually ransacked and closed around 1569. John Holubka, the last parish priest, buried the remaining church valuables and legal documents and deeds in an iron box near the vandalized church. Legal proceedings by the Catholics to get these items back were unsuccessful because no one knew where they were buried exactly. But in 1608, Mary appeared to miraculously intervene in the matter by appearing at the church and holding the baby Jesus in her arms and weeping bitterly. The apparition was on the site of the buried valuables and documents, leading to the recovery of the deed, the reclaiming of the church land by the Catholics, and the conversion of many Calvinists. Public veneration was approved in 1755 by Pope Pius VI.[45]

However, those scenarios could be deemed as anecdotal for the most part. Private miracles could happen, but there is no possible way for the person to prove that it truly happened and no possibly way for the atheist next to them to prove it truly never happened.

That is, however, unless tens of thousands of people saw a miracle of some sort. In theory, if thousands and thousands of people saw something that could not have possibly been the result of anything other than God, then God exists. This reality existed during the Miracle of the Sun.

On October 13, 1917, in Fatima, Portugal, Mary supposedly appeared to three little children and prophesied that something would happen later that day. "In October I will perform a miracle so that all may believe."[46] Seventy thousand anxious people watched and waited for something to happen.[47] The Sun then began to spin and shot toward the earth before returning to its place in the sky. A nonbeliever might state, "But, Parker, that source is from a Catholic site. Therefore it's not credible through possible bias." That's fair, so let's look at the newspaper from that day. This is not from a Catholic source; it's from the very anti-Catholic Portugal newspaper:

> "Before the astonished eyes of the crowd, whose aspect was biblical as they stood bare-headed, eagerly searching the sky, the sun trembled, made sudden incredible movements outside all cosmic laws—the sun "danced" according to the typical expression of the people."

Many supposed "debunkers" will bring up the fact that when someone looks at the Sun for a period, it will start to look like a mix of different colors. However, this argument is refuted by simply looking at the Sun. Yes, after a while, you will start to see different colors. What is not seen is "the Sun spinning, revolving 'vertiginously' on its axis" and then zigzagging toward the earth as if it had become unfixed from the Heavens' as quoted in a newspaper that day.[48] Furthermore, seventy thousand will not see that same effect. Seventy thousand people do not hallucinate all at once and see the same thing. The Miracle of the Sun goes beyond any scientific explanation.

Biblical Atrocities

There are certain atrocities in the Bible (mostly the Old Testament) that need to be addressed when defending the God of the Bible. These atrocities have been cited by atheists as proof that the Bible is not the inspired Word of God. Either that, or God is not the moral high ground that Christians claim Him to be. But as I will prove soon, these analyses do not hold up when looking at the context and history of the supposed "atrocious" biblical stories.

We know that God is the standard of good in the world. I discuss this further in a later chapter, but morality doesn't work for a variety of reasons if it is merely up to one's interpretation. Therefore, God is the moral high ground. So for an atheist to even make the argument that "God did this, therefore He is immoral" wouldn't make much sense. It may violate your subjective view of morality, but who cares? Why should your subjective morality trump God's morality?

The argument against this would be: "God says not to murder, then He told Moses to kill the Canaanites, so it's a problem for Christian philosophy. If God is hypocritical, He does not know everything. Therefore, He is not God." But as I will prove later, it is not hypocritical for God to say this in context.

First and foremost, is it immoral for God to "kill" people? I think a better question would be "Is it immoral for people to die?" If God exists, He gives us all life. God is where life comes from. So when Grandma dies of old age, did God kill her? If the answer to that is no, is the same philosophy applied to Herod's soldiers when they were washed away by the Red Sea? If the answer to the first question was yes, but the second one was no, why is that? Either God kills everyone or He kills no one. But "kill" would not be the right verb here. God does not kill anyone. Rather, He decides when you die. I cannot kill my father tomorrow, but if God wants Him to die of a heart attack that same day, it is not murder. Since we are not God, we do not get to decide who lives and who dies. Therefore, it is not hypocritical for God to say "Do not murder" and then decide that someone should die of a heart attack.

For now, let's ignore the atrocities by humans that God allows in the Bible. I will address those later in the chapter. Let's look at the first supposed atrocity by God through His power; that is, Noah's flood.

To review Genesis, God created Adam and Eve, then the descendants eventually sinned so far from God that He decided to wipe out everyone in the world with a massive flood, except for Noah and his family (people who actually followed God's command). As I have already shown earlier, it was not immoral for God to do this. God decides who lives and who dies, and if God wants to flood the world, that's up to Him. Moreover, if God wants this massive amount of people to die, that is up to Him as well. Again, it would be immoral for me to do it. But God decides who lives and who dies. Thus, if God wants these people to die because of the ripple effect, that is what He will do.

However, the follow-up question would be: "While I don't understand why your God killed that amount of people at one time, I can understand the ripple effect that your God may see. But if your God needed to kill those people (for whatever reason), why not just 'poof' them out of existence? You say your God is a God of love, but He flooded people for no reason when He could have just as easily made their suffering null and void and killed them without a flood."

Keep in mind, in the Bible it does not say, "God wiped out these people with a flood. He flooded them and did not use poof them out of existence for these reasons." This analysis is merely speculative. As I said earlier, the moral high ground cannot be objectively morally wrong. If God exists, you cannot possibly go, "I disagree with the omniscient being's morality." So, what God did cannot be objectively immoral.

But the question still remains: why did He do it this way? As I stated earlier, there had to be a specific reason that God did it in this manner. We are not God, so we cannot look at the ripple effect of just "poofing" these people out of existence. Could it be that without a massive flood, there would be massive ramifications in the future? We don't know. However, if an omniscient being exists, we need to trust Him. This argument is not that God exists. Rather, it is that given He exists, He is not a moral monster. Proving the existence of God is something that I do in later chapters. Furthermore, how is God immoral for punishing sin? What is the ideal alternative for atheists, God lets sin go unpunished like a neglectful parent?

Possibly the most well-known story in the Bible is when Moses led the Israelites out of Egypt and into the promised land. There are a few supposed moral atrocities that happened during this time. Keep in mind when analyzing these events that the Israelites needed to get out of Egypt. If they do not, Jesus would have never been born. The Israelites needed to be free in order for Jesus to have been born the way that He did. Otherwise, Jesus may have been a slave that was never able to spread His message. Or more importantly, die on the cross, saving mankind from their sins.

First, when Moses asked Pharaoh to let the Israelites go, he said no over and over again. Each time he said no, there was another plague in Egypt. This was done as a punishment of not doing what God wanted. The plagues are as follows:

I. Turning water into blood
II. Frogs everywhere
III. Lice everywhere
IV. Flies everywhere
V. Dead cattle
VI. Boils on the Egyptians
VII. Thunder, hail, and fire
VIII. Locusts everywhere
IX. Darkness
X. Firstborns are killed

Before analyzing these plagues, it's vital to ask this question: is it immoral for God to punish people for their sins? Should God let everyone into Heaven with no purification with no exceptions? Certainly not. A loving God cannot let sin go unpunished. Much like a loving parent cannot let their kids go unpunished if they aren't acting according to Christian moral values. Why even act the way Jesus wants us to if we will be eternally rewarded in Heaven regardless?

The idea that God can let sin go unpunished is absolutely asinine. The question then becomes "When did He go too far?" Look at parents for example. If a kid pushes another kid, the parent of that kid will surely punish him. What should the punishment be? Maybe the parent will restrict TV or make the kid go to bed without snacks. It's obviously completely dependent upon the parents and the child. I don't think anyone would argue that these punishments are "too harsh." But what if the parents kill the child? Is that too far? Of course it is, and no one in their right mind would argue otherwise.

But this is not the same thing. Pharaoh knew that God's chosen people were held captive in Egypt. He was told over and over again to let them go or there would be consequences. The Israelites needed to leave. There was no other option. God needed to make it happen. It's also important to note that God didn't start with killing people. He turned water into blood, put frogs everywhere, and down the list. What is God to do in this situation other than raise the punishment each time? After the blood water, was God supposed to go "Well, I guess this won't happen. Mankind is screwed because Jesus will never be born. Oh well!" Again, let me stress, this emigration *needed* to happen. So when God continued to increase the punishment, he was subconsciously telling Pharaoh, "Hey, this is going to keep getting worse if you don't allow my people to leave. You need to let them go."

"Okay I get that, but God took it too far. He didn't need to murder the Egyptians. Pharaoh would have let the Israelites go without that." Really? How do you know? God sent those nine other plagues, and each time Pharaoh went, "Is that all you got? I'm keeping these slaves." Atheists focus too much on the killing of the firstborn and don't focus on why God needed the Israelites free in the first place. Moreover, they do not look at the increasing plagues that led up to the murder. Had Pharaoh gave in after the bloody water, nothing else would have happened. But he didn't. God would not have gone to

CATHOLIC GOD, TRUE GOD

the tenth plague if He didn't know it was absolutely necessary. After all, if the God of the Bible is the true God, then He is omniscient. In order to say, "God took it too far," you'd have to know that Pharaoh would have given in at a point less severe than that. No one can know that for certain other than God. It would stand to reason that this was the least severe way that God could have made the freeing happen.

"But if God knew that Pharaoh wouldn't give in until the last plague, why not start with that? Why waste any time with essentially useless plagues?" It is the same reason that God does not exclusively create people who will believe in Him. He gives us a chance to say yes to His grace even though He knows that some will not. This is the same with Pharaoh. God gave Him the opportunity to say yes, several times, and each time he refused. As a result, God needed to up the ante.

After Pharaoh finally let the Israelites go, he changed his mind. He chased the Israelites after they had already left. I addressed the parting of the Red Sea in the second chapter. Now I want to address another thing. Was it immoral for God to drown the Egyptians in the Red Sea? A better question would be "Without interfering with free will, was there a more moral way for the Egyptians to stop pursuing the Israelites?" Again, if the God of the Bible exists, He is all-knowing. Therefore, He would know if there was a less evil way to stop the Egyptians. In order to say, "God should have done this instead," you have to imply that you know more than an all-knowing being. Which is to say, at the very least, is…well…stubborn. But is there another way that the Egyptians stop pursuing the Israelites? Probably not.

Think of it this way: if God somehow stopped the Egyptians from chasing the Israelites at that point (however He did it), what is stopping the Egyptians from attempting to get to the Israelites again? Moses and the Israelites would have to deal with that again and again. And as we have illustrated with the plagues, Pharaoh is quite stubborn. He most likely would have continued going after the Israelites again and again until he passed. Why not speed it up? Why not kill them now instead of making the Israelites deal with the Egyptians forever? The Egyptians would have died anyway. So why is it immoral? There's a very quick answer: it isn't. It isn't immoral for God to kill the Egyptians, so they can't kill/enslave the Israelites so the Israelites can get to the promised land and bring Jesus who will save all of mankind.

It's sort of like a moral dilemma you will see online. You are by the train tracks with a lever that switches the train to a different track. Track A has ten people tied to it. Track B has one person tied to it. The train is currently on track A. Forget legality for a second. Is it immoral to switch the train to track B? In doing so, you spare ten lives for the life of one. Most people would switch the tracks even if it's an overwhelmingly difficult decision.

Now imagine a different scenario. This is just a thought experiment, so it won't be very realistic. Imagine that on track A, you have an ancestor of Jesus—the man who saved all of mankind from their sins and allowed us into Heaven. If He is never born, mankind is never saved.

On track B, you have the Egyptians. They are pursuing Jesus's ancestors, trying to enslave them. The train is currently on track A. Is it immoral to switch the tracks in order to save Jesus's ancestor (thus, all of mankind) even if it means killing a few Egyptians? If not, then it was not immoral for God to do what He did in the Red Sea. If it were, you would have to explain why the lives of those specific Egyptian slave owners supersede the ability for all of mankind to go to Heaven. In short, it was not immoral for God to kill the Egyptians in the Red Sea. Rather, it was the only way for God to get what He needed to happen with free human creatures.

Like any group of people, you need a set of rules. Moses and the Israelites got these rules from God supposedly. But some say the punishment for violating these rules went a bit too far. People who refused to obey the rules were put to death. For example, here is an excerpt from the book of Leviticus:

> "The Lord said to Moses, "Say to the Israelites: 'Any Israelite or any alien living in Israel who gives any of his children to Molech must be put to death. The people of the community are to

stone him. I will set my face against that man and I will cut him off from his people; for by giving his children to Molech, he has defiled my sanctuary and profaned my holy name. If the people of the community close their eyes when that man gives one of his children to Molech and they fail to put him to death, I will set my face against that man and his family and will cut off from their people both him and all who follow him in prostituting themselves to Molech. I will set my face against the person who turns to mediums and spiritists to prostitute himself by following them, and I will cut him off from his people. Consecrate yourselves and be holy, because I am the Lord your God. Keep my decrees and follow them. I am the Lord, who makes you holy. If anyone curses his father or mother, he must be put to death. He has cursed his father or his mother, and his blood will be on his own head. If a man commits adultery with another man's wife—with the wife of his neighbor—both the adulterer and the adulteress must be put to death. If a man sleeps with his father's wife, he has dishonored his father. Both the man and the woman must be put to death; their blood will be on their own heads. If a man sleeps with his daughter-in-law, both of them must be put to death. What they have done is a perversion; their blood will be on their own heads. If a man lies with a man as one lies with a woman, both of them have done what is detestable. They must be put to death; their blood will be on their own heads.

"'If a man marries both a woman and her mother, it is wicked. Both he and they must be burned in the fire, so that no wickedness will be

73

among you. If a man has sexual relations with an animal, he must be put to death, and you must kill the animal. If a woman approaches an animal to have sexual relations with it, kill both the woman and the animal. They must be put to death; their blood will be on their own heads. If a man marries his sister, the daughter of either his father or his mother, and they have sexual relations, it is a disgrace. They must be cut off before the eyes of their people. He has dishonored his sister and will be held responsible. If a man lies with a woman during her monthly period and has sexual relations with her, he has exposed the source of her flow, and she has also uncovered it. Both of them must be cut off from their people. Do not have sexual relations with the sister of either your mother or your father, for that would dishonor a close relative; both of you would be held responsible. If a man sleeps with his aunt, he has dishonored his uncle. They will be held responsible; they will die childless. If a man marries his brother's wife, it is an act of impurity; he has dishonored his brother. They will be childless. Keep all my decrees and laws and follow them, so that the land where I am bringing you to live may not vomit you out. You must not live according to the customs of the nations I am going to drive out before you. Because they did all these things, I abhorred them.'

"But I said to you, 'You will possess their land; I will give it to you as an inheritance, a land flowing with milk and honey.' I am the Lord your God, who has set you apart from the nations. You must therefore make a distinction between clean and unclean animals and between unclean and clean birds. Do not defile yourselves by any animal or bird or anything that moves along the ground—those which I have set apart as unclean for you. You are to be holy to me because I, the Lord, am holy, and I have set you apart from the nations to be my own. A man or woman who is a medium or spiritist among you must be put to death. You are to stone them; their blood will be on their own heads.""

This looks bad at first, but there are a few reasons why it says this. Firstly, these are not behaviors that we should have today in the twenty-first century. As St. Paul tells the Romans, "We are not saved by the works of the law."[49] These rules were not meant for us today. Rather, these were specific rules for the Jewish people at the time. Some may still believe that it was immoral to kill people for minute sins. By today's standards, that argument would be correct. However, at the time, that was the way they dealt with things. They didn't have law enforcement, judges, jails, or anything like that. They put people to death to show that some action was not acceptable. Whether you believe it was still immoral or not, understand that this is not behavior for us now, as Paul explicitly says in his letter to the Romans multiple times. I talked about why the law changing later in the Bible is not a contradiction in the next chapter.

You really couldn't punish people any other way. As I have already shown, a loving God cannot let sin go unpunished. What else are they to do other than kill them? "Oh, a million other things," you say. "Why not do something less severe?" There are a couple of issues with that. First, think about context. These people are on a long voyage. So "grounding" them would not work. Imagine if Moses went, "Okay, you sinned. Now you're grounded for the next ten seconds… Okay, now let's go."

This punishment would essentially be the same as no punishment at all. "Well, then why not make the punishment longer? Why not 'ground' them for a longer period of time?"

There are only two possibilities that would arise from this form of punishment.

I.   The Israelites stay with the person.

Several things could arise from this, none of them being positive. One person commits a sin and the entire group has to stay until the punishment is over. This is a rather ridiculous scenario. You would also have to do this every single time someone sinned. If this was the case, the Israelites may not even get to the promised land at all. If you have to stop moving every time someone sins, you literally would never get to your destination. For reference, imagine you are leading a massive amount of people on foot somewhere. You have to stop every single time someone in the group makes a bad decision and wait for the punishment to be over. The harsher the crime, the harsher the time. Would you ever get to the destination? Probably not. That is why this punishment doesn't work.

The other scenario would be:

II.   The Israelites leave the person who sinned behind.

"Well if they couldn't stay with the person being punished, why not leave them? That would be a more moral punishment than killing them." This sounds like a salient point at first. But remember this: leaving someone by themselves with no supplies would be the same as killing them. This punishment as a more human alternative to killing the sinner doesn't work.

Since that form of punishment can't work, what about other alternatives? Why not beat the person who sinned instead of killing them? Remember this: there was no medicine at the time. A small cut could certainly kill you, let alone a beating. "Well, why not beat them to a point where it's not lethal?" I'm not sure what exactly the maximum amount of beating would occur for it not to be lethal. You would have to know what this amount is exactly in order to make this argument.

To go back to the grounding argument, you cannot ground someone for ten seconds and expect anyone to react to it/change their ways. This analogy works with beatings as well. Imagine if one of the Israelites did something sinful (for example's sake, let's say the person ate some pork). Moses takes this person, tells them not to do that anymore, and gives them a quick slap on the wrist. There is very little incentive for the person, and the rest of the Israelites, to stop eating pork. If the punishment is that inconsequential, it has no effect. Therefore, in order to make the argument that a group of Israelites should have beaten the sinner instead of killing them, you would have to do the maximum amount of beating that a person could take that would not be lethal. Not only does this include cuts but also just about anything else. If the person's leg breaks or something like that, they can no longer move with the group. As I showed earlier, this would be lethal as well. Moreover, they would have to beat the person to 99.99999999…percent perfectly, every time, for anyone to take the punishment seriously. Therefore, the "maximum beating" could not have possibly been very severe. And since the punishment is not severe, the people committing those sins have little incentive to stop. As a result, you can see why God commanded that the Israelites kill those who sin. It is the only way.

Later on, the Israelites came across people who were leaving the Israelites to worship a different God. God commands the Israelites who still trust in them to burn those cities to the ground in the book of Deuteronomy:

> "If you hear it said about one of the towns the Lord your God is giving you to live in that troublemakers have arisen among you and have led the people of their town astray, saying, "Let us go and worship other gods" (gods you have not known), then you must inquire, probe and investigate it thoroughly. And if it is true and it has been proved that this detestable thing has been done among you, you must certainly put to the sword all who live in that town. You must destroy

it completely, both its people and its livestock. You are to gather all the plunder of the town into the middle of the public square and completely burn the town and all its plunder as a whole burnt offering to the Lord your God. That town is to remain a ruin forever, never to be rebuilt.[50]"

I've already explained why God would have had to punish sin with death in the previous paragraphs. But why these sins? These people aren't affecting the Israelites at all, so why put them to death? This question has a major implication attached to it: that the people of these towns will not affect or interfere with the Israelites at all. How do we know that the Israelites would not have impacted the Israelites in any way? Maybe when the Israelites came across these cities, they would start to do some of the things they were doing—"a monkey see, monkey do" sort of thing. "How bad could these practices even be?" you ask. Do you think child sacrifice, sorcery, idolatry, incest, rape, sodomy, and murder[51] are evil? Would you want your people to be subject to that? And it's not like God commanded the Israelites to kill these people without warning. Deuteronomy 20:10 tells us that God told the Israelites to start with peace: "When you march up to attack a city, make its people an offer of peace." Violence was not the start but the very end.

The next question would be "But in the very next verse God says that these people will be forced to be slaves. Why would a loving God not only allow slavery but command it?" There could be a few reasons as to why. Firstly, know that there are different kinds of slavery. Yes, there was slavery without choice. This is easily what we think of when we hear the word "slavery." However, there is no possible way that God would condone this kind of slavery. Slavery is essential kidnapping in order to force labor (or sex). God forbids kidnapping in Exodus 21:16. Moreover, God commands that the Israelites look at their slaves as people in Exodus 21:20. There's also some theology that suggests that if God had revealed his whole will to the Israelites, they might not have obeyed him at all. This is partially why God puts parameters around things that are sinful in Leviticus (like divorce and slavery). If God forced the Israelites to change their way of living too drastically, they might have disavowed God's will entirely. Hypothetically, God *could* force the Israelites to do His will, as He does have that power. However, as I will show later in the book, that is not what a loving God would do.

Historically, slavery had different meanings. Some slaves chose to be slaves. "Why in the world would someone choose to be a slave?" you may ask. One word: debt. The slaves sold their labor in order to pay back the owner. We do this today as well. People sell their labor for money in return that can be used to pay debts and whatever else.

The other kind would be slavery as a form of a punishment. That is most likely what is happening here. The other groups became servants to the Israelites as a punishment for their sins. The other alternative would be death. As we see later in the chapter, that was the other option if they refused to be servants. This same thought pattern can be taken to Exodus 21:7. Again, sin cannot go unpunished, so this was not punishment without cause.

The punishment is death for a bunch of other things, but why is rape only punishable by fifty shekels of silver?[52] Shouldn't God punish that crime more severely? I agree that raping someone is more intense of a crime than disobeying one's parents for example. But we need to look at historical context. Women couldn't own property or get a job. She also had no legal protection if she didn't have a male in her life. Moreover, if an unmarried woman wasn't a virgin, it was extremely difficult for her to get married. If you put the man to death, it doesn't solve the problem of her not being able to find a husband. If you put the man to death and leave the woman (who is now not a virgin), she is now forced into slavery or prostitution.[53] But because of the punishment God set up, the woman is paid because of it. This is a *much* better situation for the woman who was raped. Not only that, but the man is forced to provide for her for the rest of his life because of his action. This is not an unjust punishment. Rather, it is the ideal punishment for the rapist and the ideal scenario for the woman who was raped.

One of the most famous "atrocities" in the Bible was the killing of the Canaanites. God details what the Israelites are to do when they see the Canaanites in Deuteronomy 7:1–6:

> "When the Lord your God brings you into the land you are entering to possess and drives out before you many nations—the Hittites, Girgashites, Amorites, Canaanites, Perizzites, Hivites and Jebusites, seven nations larger and stronger than you—and when the Lord your God has delivered them over to you and you have defeated them, then you must destroy them totally. Make no treaty with them, and show them no mercy. Do not intermarry with them. Do not give your daughters to their sons or take their daughters for your sons, for they will turn your children away from following me to serve other gods, and the Lord's anger will burn against you and will quickly destroy you. This is what you are to do to them: Break down their altars, smash their sacred stones, cut down their Asherah poles and burn their idols in the fire. For you are a people holy to the Lord your God. The Lord your God has chosen you out of all the peoples on the face of the earth to be his people, his treasured possession."

So God commands the Israelites to wipe out these people completely. This could mean that they killed them all. But look at the next verse: "Do not intermarry with them." Why would God even say this? If you killed them all, how could you intermarry with them? That would be like Hitler saying, "We are going to kill every person of Jewish descent. After we are done with that, you are not allowed to marry a Jew." You can't marry a Jew if they are all dead. Not only that, but these killings needed to happen. The Israelites needed to get to the promised land. If a group of people was in their way, they needed to be taken out.

As terrible as that sounds, go back to the Egyptian/Jesus/train analogy. Would you pull the lever and kill these people in order to save all of mankind? If you answered yes, then what God commanded here was not immoral. After all, what is the alternative? He commands that the Israelites reject war, accept defeat, and never bring the promised Messiah. That is a much worse alternative than what actually happened. Therefore, God made a good moral decision.

The last instance of a supposed atrocity in the Bible that I want to address was when Elisha commanded that God put a curse on boys for making fun of him for being bald. The story is detailed in 2 Kings 2:23–24:

> "From there Elisha went up to Bethel. As he was walking along the road, some boys came out of the town and jeered at him. "Get out of here, baldy!" they said. "Get out of here, baldy!" He turned around, looked at them and called down a curse on them in the name of the LORD. Then two bears came out of the woods and mauled forty-two of the boys."

These verses have had Christians scratching their heads for years. Why would a loving God send bears to attack kids for making fun of a bald man? Well, for one, this story could all be metaphorical. There's a possibility that this story never actually happened, and the story itself is a lesson for Christians reading it. Some Christians analyze this story in that way.[54]

But let's say that this story actually happened. These boys were actually mauled for making fun of the prophet Elisha. Firstly, when the boys said, "Get out of here," it was not so innocent as "I don't like you, so leave me." It meant, "I want you dead." We can infer this because Elijah had just been taken up to Heaven. That is what these boys wanted. They wanted Elisha dead.

It's also worth noting that we don't actually know the ages of these boys. The Hebrew translates to "youths." Obviously, toddlers would be considered youths. But it's hard to argue that these boys were toddlers. What if the boys were around the age of sixteen? Would they still be considered youth? We cannot possibly say that these boys were not of this age. We can also assume that these boys are older since God will not punish a small child who does not know right from wrong. Therefore, the boys in the story are old enough to know right and wrong. They are not little kids.

Imagine a group of forty-two sixteen-year-old boys come up to you and say, "We want you dead." Would it be immoral for God to save you? In Elisha's case, he was saved so he could bring God's Word back to the Israelites. Had God not intervened, what would've happened? Would Elisha have been killed? Would the Israelites ever turn back to God? Would Jesus have been born? Again, we don't know. But we do know that keeping Elisha safe and alive was vital to God's plan to save mankind. Therefore, we can assume that if God had not killed those boys, they would have killed Elisha and stopped the Word of God from spreading. But much more importantly, Jesus may have never been born and saved mankind. Not only that, but these boys would have most likely not lived much longer anyway. The medication at the time did not allow for a very long life expectancy. So God is essentially killing someone who would have died in a few years anyway so the Messiah could be sent.

"But God could have done it another way," you argue. "If Elisha got killed by those boys, Jesus could have come a different way." That's making a massive assumption. The only way that God could have done this is by:

I. Calling another Israelite to preach to the other Israelites about God. This would have been massively difficult to do. Israel is overcome by idol worship. There's a possibility that Elisha was the only person who loved God at the time. If he dies, there is no person to spread the Word of God anymore.
The alternative to this is:

II. God forces His will on to people even if they do not want it. This would mean that God forces at least one Israelite (possibly more) to believe in God so His message can be spread. A loving God cannot force people to believe in Him, so this cannot work. Either God is loving or He forces people who do not believe in Him to not only start believing in Him but spread His message against their will. This is not a loving God, so this cannot happen.

Again, I bore you with the train argument. Since I have just proven that if Elisha dies, Jesus is most likely never born, we will use Jesus as the example. Would you pull the lever and kill forty-two boys and save Jesus, thus saving all of mankind? If you answered yes, then you cannot possibly say that God's decision in the bear story was immoral. If you answered no, you would have to explain why the lives of these forty-two boys were more important than the lives of the rest of mankind—a quite impossible task.

The last verse I want to focus on—and the one I will spend the least amount of focus on—is Psalms 137:9. This is more than likely the most out-of-context verse cited by atheists and other nonbelievers. It reads, "Happy is the one who seizes your infants and dashes them against the rocks."

What? At first glance, it seems as if God is not only permitting infant murder but saying that people who do that become happy.

The opposition to this verse doesn't even work since it's not even God speaking. Even if it said, "We should kill infants," this does not mean we should since this opinion does not come from God. This is another reason why God needed to create a Church. Without an objective church to tell you how to read the Bible, you could read that verse and kill babies thinking it was justified by God.

With that being said, it is the Jewish people talking in that verse of Psalms. They are currently in a war with the Babylonians in order to get back to Jerusalem. So they are essentially saying that they want to kill the infants of the people they are at war with so the war can be over. It's a metaphor that the Jewish people wanted to go back to Jerusalem. The only way to do that was to win the war. This is not a verse that should be read by itself without context and is certainly not an excuse for religious people to kill infants.

There are other supposed atrocities in the Bible that could be taken out of context. Because the book does not focus on these, I do not want to defend them any further. There are other books that focus on this aspect of the Bible it its entirety.[55] I would encourage you to read those. I just wanted my readers to get a better sense of God's moral law and explain the supposed unexplainable Bible passages. Nonetheless, these verses alone show that God was not morally inaccurate when He commanded these things. Rather, He was acting in a just way.

Bible "Contradictions"

It's vital that I talk about the how the Bible does not contradict itself whatsoever. All of the supposed "contradictions" I will be talking about in this chapter are apparent disagreements and not actual disagreements. The Bible is the Word of God,[56] and it does not have discrepancies.

First and foremost, I want to reiterate that there being an Old and New Covenant is not contradictory. When God says that you must do something to be saved, let's say, being circumcised,[57] then Paul says that we are not saved by works of the law.[58] This is not a contradiction. After all, the Old Covenant is obsolete.[59] The covenant in the Old Testament was relevant at the time, but it was not relevant when Jesus came.

There are also verses in the New Testament that appear to be contradictory when it comes to salvation. You have verses like Romans 10:13 where Paul says that all who call upon the name of the Lord are saved, but in Matthew 7:21, Jesus says that not everyone who says "Lord, Lord" will enter the kingdom of Heaven but only those who do the will of His Father. It's vitally important to look at the verb tense in Paul's letter to the Romans. People who call upon the name of the Lord time and time again will be saved. This is vitally important because Paul is not saying, "Those who have called upon the name of the Lord at one point will be saved." Rather, he is saying that those who call upon the name of the Lord on a regular basis will be saved. Jesus does not contradict this because saying "Lord, Lord" does not constitute salvation by itself once. This is not a contradiction. Rather, Paul saying that you must call upon the name of the Lord throughout your life and Jesus saying that it is not enough to merely call Him Lord on occasion. You must mean it—and we show that we mean it through action.

There is a verse in Exodus that claims to show that God changes over time.[60] This cannot be. After all, if God changes His mind, then He is not all-knowing, correct? This seems like a contradiction. But it's important to know from what perspective the book of Exodus is being taken from. When Moses wrote the Pentateuch, it was taken from his point of view.[61] So from his point of view, it seemed like he changed God's mind. From our point of view, this is similar for Christians as well when we pray. We cannot change God's mind. He knows what we are going to ask. We cannot change God's mind (but that doesn't negate the effect of prayer). But from our perspective, that is what seems to be happening. That is what Moses is describing.

The next verses that claim to show that God can change is when it says God does not stay angry forever in Micah 7:18, but that He does stay angry forever in Jeremiah 17:4. Which is it? Does God stay angry forever or not? In the book of Micah, Micah says that God is merciful and forgives sin. This verse really cannot be taken any other way. Jeremiah 17:4 can be taken a couple of different ways, however. Firstly, when it says "forever," there's a possibility that it isn't even literal. "I'm going to be angry forever" could be symbolic of a very long time. A sort of "dramatic orientation," if you will. This analysis of the verse seems to be the most conducive to reality.[62] After all, Judah doesn't exist anymore, so how could God possibly still be angry at them? We cannot be angry toward someone/something that literally does not exist. It would stand to reason that when Jeremiah says God will be angry "forever," he is being dramatic and merely means, "a long time." The only other possibility is that God is still angry at a group of people that do not exist anymore.

This sort of exaggeration happens other times in Scripture as well. In the book of Ecclesiastes, the author says that the earth lasts forever.[63] But in 2 Peter 3:10, Peter makes clear that the earth will not exist one day. This is not a contradiction either. After all, the author is just saying the earth will still be here after generations pass. He cannot not be saying "forever" in a literal sense because he cannot possibly know that.

The next instance of God supposedly "changing" is in the book of Isaiah when God says He is weary in the beginning of the book[64] then says He cannot tire later in the book.[65] But we need to look at what the word "tired" means in the former context. People can get tired of things that have nothing to do with sleep. For instance, I am tired of doing the dishes every day at my current day job. This has nothing to do with slumber. It just means that I do not want to do it anymore. In the same way, God can get "tired" of someone refusing to confess sin. That is what is happening at the beginning of the book. God, a perfect being, cannot get "tired." He does not need naps. But He can get "tired" of people not confessing sin. Again, this is not the same "tired" as someone who needs to go to sleep, for example. This is just God saying that He does not want to bear the sins of the Israelites anymore. He wants them to confess their sins. Therefore, this is not a contradiction either. Isaiah is talking about two different kinds of "tired" in his book.

Another instance of God seeming to change is when it says that we cannot see God ever but also gives examples of people seeing God.[66] What does this mean? Well, we can never see God in His full glory. Meaning, we cannot even comprehend a being that knows everything, for instance. So we cannot fully "see" God in that sense. We also cannot fully "see" God because He is a spirit and has no body. But God can reveal Himself in certain ways to us. For instance, God revealed Himself to us as a human as Jesus. The people that saw Jesus saw God because Jesus is fully God (along with being fully man). God the Father can also reveal Himself to us like He did to Moses and Abraham for example. But that would have only been a spirit, so they would not have seen the face of God (again, because God does not have a face). And they could not have seen God in all of His glory because that is impossible for humans.

There are also some apparent inconsistencies involving Jesus during His time on earth. Let's start with Jesus' earthly life. How many blind men did Jesus meet when leaving Jericho? A couple of Gospels say one[67] whereas earlier it says there were two.[68] Is this a contradiction?

Well, think of it this way: If I say there were two people in a room with me—a male named Joseph and a female named Maureen—then later I say that I was in a room with Joseph, then later that I was in a room with a male, are these contradictory statements? Of course not! Earlier, I am saying that there are two people in a room. Later, I am describing one of the people. This does not mean that the other person is not there. They are just not referenced. The Gospel that says there were two men do not contradict the verses that say, "There was a man sitting there" because it does not say, "There was only one man sitting there." It is simply them saying that there was a man there, not that there was only one.

The other "inconsistency" involving Jesus's life was when He was driving the merchants from the temple. Did He curse the fig tree before[69] or after[70] driving the merchants from the temple? It's vital to understand that Matthew is speaking in a chronological order whereas Mark is not. Mark is merely saying that these two events happened. Matthew is telling them in the order that they happened. If I say, "I went to school, then went to work on Tuesday," then later say, "I went to work and school on Tuesday," this isn't an inconsistency. One is in consecutive order, the other is not.

There's also supposed inconsistences regarding the historicity of the Gospels. One of the most famous contentions is that there was not a census at the time of Jesus as the Bible depicts. However, this notion isn't true whatsoever. Or at the very least, there's no reason to believe there was no census. Wayne Brindle, professor of biblical studies, had this to say about the census: "Many censuses were taken in the Roman Empire during the time of Augustus, and there is no reason why Herod might not have been asked to take one, especially in light of conditions near the end of his life."[71] There does not seem to be positive proof of a census. Even so, there is no reason to contest that there was no census during the time.

There are other seemingly "inconsistencies" in the Bible that get the order of things different. For one, two Gospels talk about the temple curtain ripping after Jesus dies.[72] Another Gospel talks about the curtain ripping before Jesus dies.[73] This is similar to the last example. The Gospel writers are just writing in different ways.

CATHOLIC GOD, TRUE GOD

Luke is not writing in a chronological sense. We know that Matthew is, however. That must mean it is chronological in Mark's Gospel even if it is not apparent by the text (as he is just saying both things happened, and not in any order).

When Jesus was dying on the cross, He had the two thieves next to Him. One was to His right; the other was to His left. We know that one of them asked Jesus for forgiveness.[74] But in other Gospels, it says that both of them ridiculed Jesus.[75] Which one is it? This "discrepancy" cited by non-Christians fails because it assumes that once you make fun of someone, you cannot realize your wrongdoings and ask for forgiveness later on. Most likely what happened when Jesus was dying on the cross was that both thieves mocked Him. But then, one thief had a change of heart and asked Jesus to remember him when He entered His kingdom. This is not a contradiction but, rather, a different analysis of the same event.

After Jesus died, the Christian belief is that He rose from the dead, and that the tomb where He was buried was empty. All of the Gospels account for this, but they don't seem to agree on how it happened. For instance, in Matthew's Gospel, it says that an angel came down and moved the tomb.[76] In Luke's Gospel, it says that the stone covering the tomb was rolled away.[77] People mistakenly put this as a contradiction because one is not in chronological order. What Matthew seems to be doing is essentially going back in time to explain how the stone moved. It was not Jesus; He was already gone. Matthew never uses transitional words like "after" in this part of his Gospel. He says that the women went to the tomb and that there was an earthquake with an angel coming down and moved it. Most people today would view that as a contradiction, but it seems to me that Matthew is simply "going back in time" and describing how it happened. All in all, you simply can't paint this off as a contradiction because Matthew never makes it clear he is speaking chronologically. Moreover, when you compare it to the other Gospels, it seems evident that the tomb was already rolled away. This would mean that Matthew is most likely speaking in a nonchronological sense since he does not make it clear. Again, if one author says A then B happened, and another author says B and A happened, this is not a contradiction. This is merely a different way of talking.

After Jesus was done with His earthly ministry, He ascended into Heaven under His own power.[78] But was He the only person to ascend? After all, in 2 Kings 2:11, Jeremiah says that Elijah was taken up in a whirlwind to Heaven. This has to be a contradiction, right? It's important to look at word usage in the two passages. Elijah was taken up; Jesus took Himself up. This is a vitally important distinction. John is saying that no one can ascend to Heaven by his own power, not that people can't be taken to Heaven without dying. John is saying that no one can ascend to Heaven without the power of Jesus, and Elijah was taken to Heaven with the power of Jesus. There is no contradiction here.

There are also some supposed contradictions involving the Old Testament and the Israelites. The first supposed contradiction comes in the book of Genesis. The first chapter says that the humans were created after the animals[79] whereas the second chapter says the humans were created before the animals.[80] These verses need a linguistic analysis. Like other examples, it's important to note that Genesis 2 is not in chronological order. There are some Bible translations that make the language sequential. However, the original Hebrew is not in chronological order. It merely says that God formed the animals and humans, but it does not say in which order. Genesis 2 is more concerned with details than Genesis 1. Genesis 1 has more to do with sequence. Therefore, this is not a contradiction.

An important distinction in the Bible is whether or not people are punished for the sins of their fathers. Deuteronomy 5:9 says they are, but that is seemingly contracted later in that same book in Deuteronomy 24:16 when it says they are not. Before studying these verses, it's vital to see which sins are being referred to in each passage. Deuteronomy 5:9 is talking about idol worship, and Deuteronomy 24:16 is talking about general sin. This is important because God knew that if the Israelites became idol worshippers, they would fall into apostasy and reject God in future generations.[81] The children of the idol worshippers did not get sent to Hell merely for being the child of an idol worshipper. However, God knew that the children of the idol worshippers would more than likely continue the practice and be sent to Hell for it. That is why idol worshipping is stressed as a grave sin. Contrary to the atheistic analysis of Deuteronomy 5:9, children of idol worshippers are not punished simply for being descendants of idol worshippers. The response to this is usually "But it says God is jealous in that verse! This would imply that the sons of the idol worshippers were punished for no good reason because of God's jealousy." It's important to know what the word "jealousy" means. To be jealous means to want something that you do not have. God desires us all to come to Him. So in a sense, He is jealous of the idol that people worship instead of Him. This does not imply that the descendants were punished unjustly. This just means that God would be jealous of the potential idol worship that they might be doing.

Late in the Bible, it talks about how many valiant men could draw the sword for Israel. One verse says it's a total of 800,000 in Israel and 500,000 in Judah.[82] Then in a later book, it says there is a total of 1,100,000 men in Israel and 470,000 in Judah.[83] Who is correct, and why are the numbers inconsistent? Well, even though the numbers are different, that does not mean there is a substantial contradiction here. Why is this? Well, they had different methods of counting able-bodied men. In the report in 2 Samuel, the number of brave men did not include the standing army of 288,000 described in 1 Chronicles 27:1–15 or the 12,000 described in 2 Chronicles 1:14. If you include these numbers, there is a total of 1,100,000 men from Israel, so no contradiction there. Also, the 470,000 number in 1 Chronicles 21 did not include the 30,000 men of Judah mentioned in 2 Samuel 6:1. Both numbers are correct according to how they counted the number of brave men.[84]

There are too many apparent biblical inconsistencies to go through them all. That could be an entire book in of itself. But all of those "errors" are supposed errors and not real errors. A brief analysis of the verses in question show that the authors were talking about the same thing in different ways and not two antonymous things/events.

A Scientific Argument for God: How Did We Get Here?

It's rather vital that I make arguments for God from science. With all this "science contradicts God" talk going around, this is something I must address. Contrary to popular belief, science does not debunk God. At the very least, science says that God *can* exist or that He probably does. Do not take that probability lightly, however. The chances of everything in our universe existing exactly as it does is miniscule, and any variation of that results in no human race. With that being said, I will be going through scientific arguments for the existence of God and proving that without God, the chances of everything happening in the universe the way it did is fiercely minute.

Before getting into the many arguments from science, I want to address one contrary: science disproves (or contradicts evidence of) God. As you will see, this proposition is vastly untrue. But what better way to prove that point than to show quotes from the most prominent scientists of all time?

> "This most beautiful system of the sun, planets and comets, could only proceed from the counsel and dominion of an intelligent and powerful Being." (Sir Isaac Newton)[85]

> "The impossibility of conceiving that this grand and wondrous universe, with our conscious selves, arose through chance, seems to me the chief argument for the existence of God." (Charles Darwin)[86]

"I find it as difficult to understand a scientist who does not acknowledge the presence of a superior rationality behind the existence of the universe as it is to comprehend a theologian who would deny the advances of science." (Wernher von Braun)[87]

I could cite even more. Not every scientist believes in God, but that isn't really an issue for this argument. Certainly some, like Charles Darwin, are vehemently against a personal God. I am not attempting to prove the existence of God through science (at least, not yet). I am merely trying to prove that science cannot possibly disprove God. If it disproved God, then no scientists would be theist. Being that some scientists are religious means that science can—in no way, shape, or form—"disprove" God.

I am also not a major fan of the "God of the gaps" argument. For those unaware, this philosophy has been known to throw God into any sort of scientific unknown. This has dwindled down more as we come to understand the world better (i.e., we can't attribute lightning bolts to "God's wrath" anymore, as we know the science behind it).

Saying "It can only be God" is a rather unscientific argument for that reason. But saying "It can't possibly be God" is much worse. I can understand not viewing lightning as "God's wrath," but it's rather a disservice to say that unexplained scientific phenomena cannot *possibly* be God. Saying "I don't know, but it can't be God" without sustainable proof is much worse than saying "I don't know, but I think it's God" because in the latter, you are forming a conclusion based on the world around you. In the former, you aren't forming a conclusion, but you are throwing out a possible hypothesis for no reason.

That would essentially be like a detective saying, "We don't know who committed this murder, but suspect A is our top suspect as of now. I don't know for certain, but I think it is him based of the evidence I see." The other detective comes in with the same exact evidence as the first detective, saying, "I don't know who did it, but I *know* it wasn't subject A." How do you know this? Did someone tell you? How can you trust them?

For science that we have yet to explain, we should not rule out the existence of God. This goes especially for those questions that we will most likely never have a one hundred percent testable and retestable answer.

But for theist, we should not throw God into any situation without reason. One argument I see brought up is that because the world looks so beautiful, God must exist! While I of course believe God exists, and that that God helped move natural selection along, I do not see this as a viable argument for Christians. Natural selection, as a scientific notion, is a widely accepted theory among scientists. "Look at how beautiful the world is" is not a great argument despite how much God would have intervened and continue to intervene in the evolutionary process.

With the scientific information at hand, we cannot throw out the possibility of God. For instance, we don't know where our laws of physics come from. We may never know, but to say "I know these didn't come from God" with no evidence that suggests where they came from is rather ridiculous. Moreover, it is a disfavor to the scientific method to throw out a hypothesis with no evidence to back up other hypotheses.

Where Did We Come From?

Imagine for a second that one must do everything consciously. Every heartbeat, digestion, breathing, and blinking all must be done manually. Obviously, this is not an ideal scenario. However, through anatomic nerves, we can do these things manually. This could have happened through evolution with or without God, but it's worth noting. Evolution is so perfect that it's difficult to study it without the possibility that it was all orchestrated by God. Evolution did happen and continues to happen (despite what young-earth creationists might say). All species have common ancestors of bacteria. However, evolution in its reality does not diminish any arguments for the existence of God. Evolution could have happened and been inspired by

God. Meaning, God set evolution in place to become what it is today and what it will continue to become in the future.

One argument brought up by Christians who believe in evolution is the Cambrian explosion. Around 530 million years ago, a set of bacteria came to earth in an extremely short geological time span. This period lasted about ten million years. These "phyla" also had absolutely no evidence of early ancestors, and we still have no answer as to where they came from.[88] Christians who favor evolution argue that God put the bacteria on earth and helped to minister evolution to the life-forms we know today. If not God, then where did these things come from? Of course, further scientific research could prove a common ancestor, but where did that ancestor come from?

Let's start with the scientific arguments and not just the arguments that transcend science, shall we? To start my first argument regarding the big bang, here's a scientific fact: things don't just show up. Matter doesn't just come out of nowhere. This is proven through the first law of thermodynamics. "Matter cannot be created or destroyed." For example, the elements that we know today could not have just shown up on their own. What does this have to do with God? If anything, this disproves God because if something cannot come from nothing, then no being can come from nothing, including God. If God exists, He would have to come from nothing, thus throwing the first law of thermodynamics out the window.

However, here's something to keep in mind. Let's say for example that the big bang theory is the reason that matter, space, and time all came together at once. There was an explosion that created everything as we know it today. So either nothing exploded into something or some type of matter exploded into other matter. The first one is easily debunked because nothing cannot explode. If it's truly "nothing," then it cannot do anything as it is nothing. If something exploded, this is debunked by the first law of thermodynamics. Where did that original something come from? It's also important to note that even if the big bang theory is not the true beginning of the universe, the universe would still have to have matter, space, and time come to be at once. Why is this?

If you have matter and space but no time, when would you put the matter in space? If you have matter and time but no space, there would be nowhere for matter to go. And of course, if you have time and space but no matter, there is nothing to go into space. For this reason, matter, space, and time must have all been created at the same time. Even if matter, space, and/or time were created before the creation of the known universe, the question remains: where did it come from? The big bang either exploded nothing or exploded some type of matter. Both possibilities do not make sense from a scientific standpoint.

Because of this, both realities require God. Nothing cannot explode; therefore, God created the explosion. Nothing cannot create, therefore God created. Matter also does not just appear (or explode) without something making it appear or explode. Therefore, God created the matter that exploded. The universe was either started by God or some matter that exploded without cause, without anyone making it explode, and with no scientific reasoning for that matter being there. God created the universe in its entirety. It is also rather unusual to me that some people believe that the Big Bang Theory nullifies God's existence, or even worse, disproves it entirely, given that it was a Catholic scientist that first theorized the Big Bang.[89]

Let's say someone doesn't think that the big bang theory was the beginning of the universe. I am not going to be going through every single theory in this book as that is not the purpose of this book. Regardless, if it weren't the big bang, the universe would have had to start. There would have had to have been a beginning. The universe could not have existed forever. You cannot continue to keep going back for infinity because you would never have started in the first place.

If that seems far-fetched, consider this analogy: Think about your family tree (your father's side to be specific). Your father was not the start of your family (on your dad's side anyway) because he had a father. Your grandfather could not have been the start of your family because he had a father. So on and so forth. Keep going back until scientists believe our ancestors were not truly human. Keep going further to when we were single-celled organisms. Which single-celled organism was the beginning? I don't know, and frankly it doesn't matter. One of them had to be the start for the reason above. You cannot keep going back to infinity asking the question "Is this the beginning?" if the answer is always no. If there is no start, there is nothing. This same analogy can be applied to the universe. Furthermore, because elements are the building blocks of everything we know today, one would either have to believe that the elements always existed, or that God exists. Either that, or the logical impossibility that nothing created the elements.

Because from a scientific perspective, God really cannot be disproven. One contention I have heard is that because telescopes have never seen a bearded man sitting on a cloud, God must not exist. How preposterous of a contention is this? The definition of God is that there is a timeless, spaceless, immaterial in the universe. "We can't see Him" isn't an argument at all. We know that we cannot see Him, that's His entire thing. Note: as I've talked about earlier, God can reveal Himself to us in a variety of ways. As a general rule, He is immaterial. But since He is also omnipotent, He can use His power to reveal Himself in any way, shape, or form. God also does not have a moral duty to show Himself at any time if He does not want to. After all, if God is all-knowing, He knows the implications of showing Himself and not showing Himself.

An Argument from Scientific Probability

We know why men are more subject to color blindness, but it's rather random who gets that gene. Yes, your mother must carry. But we can't tell for certain if someone is going to be color-blind simply by looking at his or her parents' genetic code. The only words we could say would be "maybe," "probably," "most likely not," among others, never "yes" or "no." I understand sometimes you will say yes or no. For example, if two parents have certain blood types, their offspring cannot *possibly* have certain kinds.

I am not talking about those scenarios. I am talking about the "maybe" scenarios. For instance, when someone has a 1/10 chance of being left-handed, where does that come in? Who gets to decide if that person is left-handed or not? Is it God? All of these questions are almost unanswerable as far as genetics go. How could you possibly throw out a hypothesis when you do not have a conclusion that contradicts that hypothesis?

When the percentages are large like that, you could say an event happened by chance. Imagine you do a random number generator and make the numbers 1–10. The chance of rolling a 4 on the first click is 10 percent. Given that the percentage is double digits, it wouldn't be a good argument to say that God made it roll a 4. And if you click it again, there is a 1 percent chance of it being a 4 again. Still, you could not attribute this to God. One percent is not an extremely small percentage. Again, you could say that this happened just by chance.

But how far are we going to take this? What about a probability that is so small it's impossible to quantify? Are we still going to say, "It all happened by chance"? Or are we going to say that some being made life the way it is? If you did that same random number generator but did 1–1 trillion, the chances of it being 6 is 1/1 trillion. Pretty rare, but the odds of doing it again with the same number would be astronomical—1/1E24 to be exact. That is one in one with 24 zeroes after. To put this into further perspective, imagine you had a die that had one million sides instead of the standard six. What are the odds that you roll a 15? It wouldn't take a mathematician to realize that those odds are one in a million. However, what are the odds that you roll 15 four times in a row? This would be $1/1,000,000^4$, or 0.00000000000000000000001%. I don't know about you, but I wouldn't be betting with those odds.

But even so, these numbers don't even compare to the statistical probability that life came on earth randomly. Two astronomers by the names of Fred Hoyle and N. Chandra Wickramasinghe have made it known that life on earth had an astronomically low chance of exist randomly. In fact, they figured out that by random trial, life would have come to earth in 1/10E40,000 times. A number so small it isn't even quantifiable by most calculators. Here's a quote from their book *Evolution from Space*:

"Life cannot have had a random beginning...
The trouble is that there are about two thousand
enzymes, and the chance of obtaining them all
in a random trial is only one part in 10 to the
40,000 power, an outrageously small probability that could not be faced even if the whole
universe consisted of organic soup. If one is not
prejudiced either by social beliefs or by a scientific
training into the conviction that life originated on
the Earth, this simple calculation wipes the idea
entirely out of court... The enormous information content of even the simplest living systems...
cannot in our view be generated by what are often
called "natural" processes... For life to have originated on the Earth it would be necessary that quite
explicit instruction should have been provided for
its assembly... There is no way in which we can
expect to avoid the need for information, no way
in which we can simply get by with a bigger and
better organic soup, as we ourselves hoped might
be possible a year or two ago.[90]"

Life on earth only exists randomly (i.e., without God)
once in every 10E40,000 times. Going back to the dice analogy
from earlier, we determined that the odds of rolling a 15 4 times
in a row on our one-million sided die was one in a trillion, or
0.0000000000000000000001%. This number does not even compare to the number calculated here. To imagine this number, imagine
you have a die that has one million sides again. The odds that you
roll a 15 every single time for 6,667 times is 1/10E40,000. That's
how crazy these probabilities are getting. There is some speculation
over where they got this number and the validity of it. However, my
argument is not that this number is correct. My argument goes into
ramifications of what we can conclude *if* this number is correct. Later
in the chapter, I will make more specific "goldilocks" arguments for
God's existence. The atheistic counter would most likely be some-

thing like "In an infinite universe, it was bound to happen some-time." You can say that, and you would most likely be correct. As the old saying goes, if you give a monkey a typewriter and an infinite amount of time to write, he will eventually write Shakespeare. And this would be a fantastic argument if, of course, the universe is infinite years old. Some scientists have said that it *could* be, which is different from the standard number I have seen that the universe is around 13.8 billion years old.[91] So the real question theists should pose is not "How do you explain the very low probability of life existing on earth?" The question that I have yet to receive a response from is "How did it happen this perfectly so early?" In 10E40,000 trials, life not only came into existence but only took around ten billion years to do so. Ten billion years is a very long time, make no mistake. But these miniscule probabilities should not be happening this early. To this, you could still say that it was all by chance—even if the probability is incomprehensibly low. But what is more likely, that we got it perfect extremely early against (to understate) overwhelming odds by random chance or that a divine being created the earth?

Now, even if atheists (by their overwhelming confirmation bias) still think that life on earth came by chance, they still have a very important question to answer: How did intelligent life not only come to be on earth in such a short period of time but flourish? A planet not only has to have certain parameters for life but has to keep those parameters for that life to flourish. Evolution may have created humans by random probability. This may be the case, considering that natural selection creates the best and brightest. The brightest would eventually evolve into what we call humans, and humans continue to evolve as we speak. We just so happen to be the only organisms with metacognition.

I don't think most people understand just how ridiculously low the chances are that earth continued to provide enough resources for us to flourish on earth (and continue to flourish). We used to believe that there were only two parameters for life to exist on a planet. You need a specific kind of star, and you need a planet that is X distance away from that star. Seems easy enough, right? The issue is not finding planets that fit these parameters. It's finding life on these planets. Because, as scientists have figured out, you need much more than these two parameters to sustain life on a planet. As astrophysicist Dr. Hugh Ross points out, there are around two hundred parameters that planets must be in the Goldilocks Zone for in order to sustain life. I will be going through many of them now.[92]

1. Galaxy cluster type
    ɔ If too rich, galaxy collisions and mergers would disrupt the solar orbit.
    ɔ If too few, there is unsatisfactory infusion of gas to sustain star formation for long enough time.
2. Galaxy size
    ɔ If too big, infusion of gas and stars would disturb sun's orbit and ignite too many galactic eruptions.
    ɔ If too little, insufficient infusion of gas to sustain star formation for long enough time.
3. Galaxy type
    ɔ If too elliptical, star formation would stop before heavy element build-up for life chemistry.
    ɔ If too irregular, radiation exposure on occasion would be too severe and heavy elements for life chemistry would not be available.
4. Galaxy mass distribution
    ɔ If there's too much mass in the central bulge, a potentially life-supportable planet will be exposed to too much radiation.
    ɔ If too much in the spiral arms, a potentially life-supportable planet will be destabilized by the gravity and radiation.
5. Galaxy location
    ɔ If too close to a rich galaxy cluster (or too close to other very large galaxies), galaxy would be gravitationally disrupted.
    ɔ If too far away from dwarf galaxies, there is an insufficient amount of gas and dust to sustain the formation of stars.

6.   Decay rate of cold dark matter particles
   - If too small, too few dwarf spheroidal galaxies will form. This prevents star formation too long for life-supportable planets become possible.
   - If too great, too many dwarf galaxies will form. This will make the orbits of solar-type stars unstable and lead to the generation of deadly radiation.
7.   Hypernova eruptions
   - If too few, not enough heavy element ashes present for the formation of rocky (life habitable) planets.
   - If too many, there would be too many collision events in planetary system.
   - If too soon or too late, it leads to a galaxy evolution history that would disturb the possibility of advanced life.
8.   Supernovae eruptions
   - If too close, too late, or too frequent, life on the planet would be exterminated by radiation.
   - If too far or too few, not enough heavy element ashes would exist for the formation of life habitable planets.
   - If too soon, heavy element ashes would be too heavily distributed for the formation of rocky planets.
9.   White dwarf binaries
   - If too few or too soon, there's not enough fluoride produced for life chemistry to proceed.
   - If too many, planetary orbits disrupted by the stellar density.
   - If too late, fluorine would be made too late.
10.   Proximity of solar nebula to a supernova eruption
   - If too far, too few heavy elements for life would be absorbed.
   - If too close, the nebula would be blown apart.

11. Timing of solar nebula formation relative to super-nova eruption
   o If too early, nebula would be blown apart.
   o If too late, nebula would not absorb enough heavy elements.

12. Number of stars in parent star birth aggregate.
   o If too few, there's insufficient input of certain heavy elements into the solar nebula.
   o If too many, planetary orbits will be too disturbed.

13. Star formation history in parent star vicinity
   o If too much too soon, planetary orbits would, again, be too radically disturbed.

14. Birth date of the star-planetary system
   o If too early, quantity of heavy elements will be too low.
   o If too late, star would not yet have reached stable burning phase.

15. Parent star distance from center of galaxy
   o If too far, the number of heavy elements would be too low to make rocky planets
   o If too close, galactic radiation would be too great and stellar density would disturb planetary orbits.

16. Parent star distance from closest spiral arm
   o If too large, exposure to harmful radiation from galactic core would be too massive

17. Z-axis heights of star's orbit
   o If more than one, tidal interactions would disrupt planetary orbit.
   o If less than one, heat produced would be insufficient for life.

18. Quantity of galactic dust
   o If too small, star and planet formation rate is inadequate.
   o If too large, there would be too many collisions in the planetary system, among other things.

19.   Number of stars in the planetary system (essentially, the number of "suns")
- If more than one, tidal interactions would disrupt planetary orbit (there's also the obvious possibility of it being too hot for life to sustain).
- If less than one, (I'm sure you can figure that one out yourself).

20.   Parent star mass
- If too great, the star would burn too rapidly.
- If too little, the range of planet distances for life would be too narrow.

21.   Planet star metallicity
- If too small, there's not enough heavy elements for life chemistry to exist.
- If too large, radioactivity would be too intense for life.

22.   Parent star color
- If too red or too blue, there wouldn't be a sufficient enough photosynthetic energy for plants.

23.   Galactic tides
- If too weak, there's too low of a comet ejection rate from giant planet region (too strong of a galactic tide has the opposite affect).

24. H_3^+ production
- If too small, simple molecules essential to planet formation and life chemistry will not form.
- If too large, planets will form at wrong time and place for life.

25.   Flux of cosmic ray protons
- If too small, inadequate cloud formation in planet's troposphere (too large of a flux has the opposite affect).

26.   Solar wind
- If too weak, there are too many clouds (too strong solar wind produces the opposite affect).

27.   Parent star luminosity relative to speciation
- If it increases too soon, a runaway greenhouse effect would develop.
- If increases too late, runaway glaciation would develop.

28.   Surface gravity
- If too strong, planet's atmosphere would retain too much ammonia and methane.
- If too weak, planet's atmosphere would lose too much water.

29.   Distance from parent star
- If too far, planet would be too cool for a stable water cycle (a planet too close would have the opposite affect).

30.   Inclination of orbit
- If too great, temperature differences would be rather extreme.

31.   Orbital eccentricity
- If too great, seasonal temperature differences also be too extreme.

32.   Axial tilt
- If greater or less than the desired range, surface temperature differences would be too great.

33.   Rate of change of axial tilt
- If greater, climatic changes would be too extreme.

34.   Rotation period
- If too long, temperature differences would be too great.
- If too short, atmospheric wind velocities would be too great.

35.   Rate of change in rotation period
- If too long or too short, surface temperature range necessary for life would not be sustained.

36. Planet age
    o If too young, planet would rotate too rapidly (a planet that is too old will have the opposite affect).

37. Magnetic field
    o If too strong, electromagnetic storms would be too severe.
    o If too weak, the ozone shield wouldn't be protected from hard stellar and solar radiation.

38. Thickness of crust
    o If too thick, too much oxygen would be transferred from the atmosphere to the crust.
    o If too thick, volcanic and tectonic activity would be too great.

39. Ratio of reflected light to total amount falling on surface
    o If too great, runaway glaciation would develop (too less would result in runaway greenhouse instead).

40. Cometary collision rate
    o If too great, too many species would become extinct.
    o If too few, crust would be too depleted of materials essential for life.

41. Oxygen to nitrogen ratio in atmosphere
    o If too large, advanced life functions would proceed too quickly (too small of a ratio produces the opposite affect).

42. Carbon dioxide level in atmosphere
    o If too great, runaway greenhouse effect would develop.
    o If too few, plants are not able to photosynthesize a sufficient amount.

43. Water vapor level in atmosphere
    o If greater, runaway greenhouse effect would develop.

          ɔ If less, rainfall would be too few and far between.

44.   Amount of oxygen in the atmosphere
- ɔ If too great, plants and hydrocarbons would burn up too easily.
- ɔ If less, pretty obvious.

45.   Nitrogen quantity in atmosphere
- ɔ If too great or too little, too much buffering of oxygen for advanced animal respiration.

46.   Volcanic activity
- ɔ If too low, insufficient amounts of carbon dioxide and water vapor would be returned to the atmosphere.
- o If too high, advanced life would be destroyed.

47.   Timing of birth of continent formation
- o If too early or too late, silicate-carbonate cycle would be destabilized.

48.   Oceans-to-continents ratio
- o If too great or too small, diversity and complexity of life-forms would be limited.

49.   Global distribution of continents (for Earth)
- o If too much in the southern hemisphere, seasonal differences would be too severe for advanced life to inhabit.

50.   Frequency and extent of ice ages
- o If too small, insufficient mineral concentrations occur for diverse and advanced life.
- o If greater, planet experiences freezing too great for life to be inhabited.

51.   Soil mineralization
- o If too few or too many nutrients, diversity and complexity of life-forms would be limited.

52.   Gravitational interaction with a moon
- o If too great, tidal effects would be too severe.
- o If too less, this would cause climatic instabilities, among other things.

53.   Jupiter distance (or another very large planet)
o   If too great (or if Jupiter's mass is too small), too many asteroid collisions would occur on Earth.
o   If too less (or if Jupiter's mass is too great), Earth's orbit would become unstable.

54.   Mass of Neptune
o   If too small, not enough Kuiper Belt Objects (asteroids beyond Neptune) would be scattered out of the solar system.
o   If too large, chaotic resonances among the gas giant planets would occur.

55.   Atmospheric pressure
o   If too small, liquid water will evaporate too easily and condense too infrequently; weather and climate variation would be too extreme; lungs will not function.
o   If too large, liquid water will not evaporate easily enough for land life; insufficient sunlight reaches planetary surface; insufficient UV radiation reaches planetary surface; insufficient climate and weather variation; lungs will not function.

56.   Iron quantity in oceans and soils
o   If smaller, quantity and diversity of life would be too limited for support of advanced life; if very small, no life would be possible.
o   If larger, iron poisoning of at least advanced life would result.

57.   Tropospheric ozone quantity
o   If smaller, insufficient cleansing of biochemical smogs would result.
o   If larger, respiratory failure of advanced animals, reduced crop yields, and destruction of ozone-sensitive species would result.

58. Stratospheric ozone quantity
    o If smaller, too much UV radiation reaches planet's surface causing skin cancers and reduced plant growth.
    o If larger, too little UV radiation reaches planet's surface causing reduced plant growth and insufficient vitamin production for animals.
59. Quantity and extent of forest and grass fires
    o If smaller, soil would be insufficient for plant life.
    o If greater, too many plant and animal life forms would be destroyed.
60. Average rainfall precipitation
    o If too small, inadequate water supplies for land-based life.
    o If too large, too much erosion of land masses.
61. Distance from nearest black hole
    o If too close, radiation will prove deadly for life.
62. Frequency of gamma ray bursts in galaxy
    o If too low, inadequate production of copper, titanium, and zinc; insufficient hemisphere-wide mass extinction events.
    o If too great, too much production of copper and zinc.
63. Parent star magnetic field
    o If too low, solar wind and solar magnetosphere will not be adequate.
    o If too great: too high of an X-ray flux will be generated.

I could have cited many more, but I decided against it, as the great majority of my audience will not even understand the large words. I wanted to use proofs that members of the general populous could visualize, not large science terms that only a minute fraction of people could understand. Keep in mind that these proofs go much, much further. The idea that this all happened by chance is unfathomable and a large reason to believe in God.

Analyzing Arguments for God

One of the most famous Catholic theologians of all time is St. Thomas Aquinas. His five proofs for the existence of God are still some of the most relevant arguments for the existence of God, even after all these years. Aquinas's proofs were one of the most pivotal parts of Christian apologetic history. Because of this, it would be greatly beneficial to go through those proofs and analyze them.

The first argument would be the argument from motion.

This argument is summarized by the following premises:

I.   Things are in motion
II.   Things are in motion because of something that put said object into motion
III.   There cannot be an infinite regress of movers
IV.   There has to be a first mover, an unmoved mover. We call this God

Aquinas argues that things that change change because of something else changing it. For instance, if I get pushed off a building, I am changed by someone in the action of pushing me. This person was influenced by something to push me. We can keep going back for infinity because everything that changes is changed because of something else. However, as Aquinas notes, how could this be? How could we be where we are today with an infinite regress? That would be asking when I would get to my friend if I was infinite miles away from him. It simply doesn't make sense.

Aquinas argues, then, that this must have been started by an unmoved mover (God).

This ties into the second proof very well. The second argument is the argument from efficient causes. Each thing is done because of something else. This can either be because you wanted to do something or you were forced to. Nonetheless, there was a cause. Along with this fact, it's worth noting that everything has a beginning. Nothing, then, can cause itself to exist. I cannot cause my existence. However, this same principle applies to every species on earth. Humans were not caused because humans wanted to exist. Because even if they had the functioning prefrontal cortex to be able to think rationally in that way, they cannot cause it themselves.

If there is no cause, there is no effect. Because of this, you need a first cause to start the universe. If there was no start/cause to the universe, it could not have come into existence. This is the most compelling argument of the five in my opinion. This was one of the best arguments I had for God when I first started debating His existence, without even realizing that it was an argument from Aquinas.

To use an example more easily understandable by the human brain, say you had an infinite number of lightbulbs on an infinitely long wire. Would one expect said light bulbs to be lit? Of course not! There is no power source. There cannot be an infinite regress of lightbulbs and wire, because then, the light bulbs could not be lit at all.

In Aquinas' proof, he makes a distinction between an accidentally ordered series (a series where one is not reliant on the first cause still existing) and an essentially ordered series (a series where the first cause is essential and always will be essential, without this first cause, nothing can come from it). Nevertheless, giving an example of an accidental series through the essential cause will also be beneficial in my argument. My parents created me, their parents created them, and so on. You can keep going back for thousands and thousands of years. Now, go back millions of years. Before my ancestors were human beings, they were different types of animals. Keep going back until you get to the one-celled organism without ancestors. What caused them to be there? Now consider that same argument with any other scientific idea. How did stars come about? What about planets? Milky ways? These are complicated questions that are very complicated to answer. Nonetheless, where is the cause? If you keep going back, you go back to the big bang, or the "start" of the universe. You need a start because if you kept going back in causes, we would not exist. If you do not have God to start the universe, it would have never started. I touched on this in my chapter arguing with science already. The big bang theory literally cannot cause itself. If it did, we would have to throw away a fundamental law of thermodynamics. Because of this, God (the first cause) was necessary in the creation of all things. Either that or the universe (and every cause) goes back to infinity. That argument makes little sense because if this were the case, you and I could not exist today. Be that as it may, a first cause is necessary and paramount in the creation of everything. What else would that be besides God?

The third proof goes like this: we find things in nature that come into existence and leave existence. Nothing that we see is always here. An appropriate assumption then would be that every being is contingent. Every contingent being has a point where it does not exist. It is impossible, then, for contingent beings to have existed at one point. So hypothetically, there could have been a time where nothing existed. If there was a point where there was nothing, we would still have nothing. Nothing cannot create the universe. If every being is a contingent being, then all we would not be here. Therefore, not every being is a contingent being.

Since there could not have been a point where there was literally nothing, it would stand to reason that a noncontingent being exists. The only other reality would be that nothing somehow expanded into…the universe? It sounds asinine when you put it together. Therefore, some being exists out if its own necessity. Moreover, if no being exists out of its own necessity, we would not have a universe. There must be a being that does not receive existence from another being. This would be nothing other than God.

The fourth proof starts off in an objective truth: we are not equal. Some people are better at some things than others. For reference, let's say we are arguing where someone is on the "good person" scale. Rapist serial killers are on the evil part of the spectrum, and those who give significant amounts to charity are on the good part of the spectrum. This is not something that is generally debated. But it's important to note: what is the standard of goodness? How could you even say that the person who gives to charity is a good person (or at least, that the charity was altruistic)? And how could you say that the serial rapist is a bad person? What is your standard of goodness, and what is your standard of evil? Now, atheists can certainly be moral. I have met several. But they cannot justify the morality of Hitler other than saying, "Murder is bad." But why? If we are all just atoms through randomized evolution with no objective moral standard and goodness, why would murder be bad? After all, we are all just cells running around until our inevitable death and decay. Why not speed up the process? Everyone (for the most part) agrees that murder is evil. However, how do we judge this? Christians can justify this morality whereas subjectivist atheists cannot. Therefore, atheists cannot possibly justify saying that Hitler was a person with bad morals or that someone who gives significant amounts to charity has good morals.

I'm sure everyone reading this would agree that the Nazi philosophy of putting people in concentration camps is evil even if they believed it to be moral. But consider this scenario: imagine that the Nazis won WWII. No one knows what the world would be like if this scenario came true. But let's imagine for a second that because the Nazis won WWII, in one hundred years or so from now, everyone agrees, universally, that what the first Nazis did was morally good. We continue to put Jewish people in concentration camps simply for being Jewish.

Does this make it morally correct? Meaning, if everyone agrees with it, is it moral? If yes, then at what number is it immoral? After all, if we are to subjugate morality to how many people agree with it, where does it become a problem? What if 10 percent of people disagree? Fifteen percent? Twenty percent? What number is it? If 80 percent of humans believe rape is moral, does that make it moral? Should we be going off mob rule to make moral decisions?

Obviously, this is ridiculous. Mob rule does not decide morality. Just because 100 percent or 90 percent or 87 percent, or whatever the percentage may be, of people agree that something is moral does not make it moral. So if humans do not get to decide what morality is, where does it come from? An all-knowing being, of course. To compare good and bad humans, you need an objective moral good. We all know this to be God.

Some atheists have said that our standard of morality has come through evolution and not God. The issue with this philosophy is that to even make this argument, you would have to accept that morality does not come from ourselves. Why is this? Well, the Christian moral argument is that we do not "make up" morality as we go along. Rather, we "discover" it. Again, if morality is subjective, we cannot "get better," objectively speaking. We can only change. Murder is evil because the objective standard outside of ourselves told us it was evil. We need to accept this moral standard and abide by it.

The fifth and final proof for the existence of God ties together the rest. Aquinas says that the human species always works toward some goal. This is not by chance. Some goals for example—like survival—are a natural biological process for everyone. Then he says that human beings lack knowledge—an uncontroversial statement. But again, how can we even know what the ultimate thing is without an all-knowing being? How do we measure the intelligent people to the non-intelligent people? The same basic argument for the fourth proof goes for this one. Comparisons do not make sense without an ultimate on either side. Obviously, an all-knowing being would be the only standard for this. If an all-doltish being exists, it doesn't know anything. It doesn't even know what it does not know. Therefore, we cannot ask what it knows. God is the standard for intelligence. God knows everything, so He is the standard for intelligence.

Aquinas's five proofs are a great way to explain the concept of God through philosophical means. They are not by themselves, however, as he expands on them greatly. For now, I will be moving to a different way of thinking about God; that is, the argument from Alvin Plantinga.

The argument goes like this: It is possible that a maximally great being exists. That is a statement that should not be debated. There is certainly a possibility that I've demonstrated at earlier points in the book. Now, if it's possible for a maximally great being to exist, then one exists in some possible world. This doesn't seem super far-fetched and doesn't seem like a super compelling argument for my side. Certainly, it's possible for God to exist in some possible world. But here's where it gets interesting. If this maximum being (God) exists in some possible world, then He exists in every possible world. The nature of God is that He is always everywhere. That is, He is omnipresent. If God exists in some possible universe, then He exists in all of them. If you deny this point, you must deny one of the first two. Because given that the first two are true, you cannot deny the third one. If the being talked about in the first two points is truly the maximally great being, then it can always be everywhere. If it cannot do something, then it is not a maximally great being, correct? Therefore, if it is possible for a maximally great being to exist in some possible world, then it exists in our world. If this is true, then a maximally great being exists. Therefore, God exists. It's an excellent way of thinking because the only way that it could be "debunked" by atheists is for them to say that there is no possible way for a maximally great being to exist in some possible universe—which would be extremely disingenuous. I talked about this in the previous chapter, but I will reiterate here. But to do the opposite is even worse. Saying "I do not know certain things about how our universe started but I know it cannot be God" is the same thing as people saying "It is the wrath of God coming down" before we understood the science of lightning bolts. Neither have proof for the claim, but the atheist argument of "Well, it can't possibly be God" is mendacious to oneself. How do you know this? You know this as a fact? Are you an all-knowing being? Well then, we should call you God. Quit being so full of yourself. We have questions about the universe. I certainly do not know the answers. But throwing out a maximum being because it impugns your own subjective worldview of what you want the universe to be because of some ridiculous confirmation bias or hatred for Christianity is even more ridiculous than I can even comprehend.

A Closer Look at
Objective Morality

The idea of free will is great because it explains many things. For one, it explains why God does not stop human evil. For another, it explains why not everyone goes to Heaven. After all, if God gives us the choice to choose between Heaven and Hell, some people will choose Hell. This is a reality even if it goes against the person's best interest. But let's go back to the human evil question. Why shouldn't God stop evil? He could—technically speaking—end all evil. Why not do it? The answer again is free will. If we cannot choose evil, then we cannot choose good and therefore have no choice in choosing God. I explain why this philosophy doesn't make sense later in the chapter. "But couldn't God stop Hitler? I understand Him not stopping someone stealing a pencil or some other small evil like that. But why not stop a larger evil like Hitler?"

The same analogy applies. If you cannot choose evil, then you cannot choose good. Moreover, if you believe God should stop evil, but not someone stealing a pencil, where is the line drawn? Each atheist would have to answer this question if they believe God should have stopped Hitler but not petty theft. Should God stop someone from killing someone? What about rape? What about lying? Should each petty lie be stopped or just the larger ones? What constitutes a large lie and a smaller one? Needless to say, there would be much ambiguity if you asked these questions in a survey.

Moreover, who's to say that God hasn't stopped some sort of evil without us knowing? Maybe if Hitler was never born (let's say miscarriage), disastrous effects ensue—yes, effects worse than the Holocaust and WWII. We can't see alternate realities, so we can't possibly know this. Keep in mind: I am not by any means saying what

CATHOLIC GOD, TRUE GOD

Hitler did was morally acceptable. It was not at all morally correct. All I am saying is that we don't know if God prevented something much, much worse by allowing Hitler to live.

Not only that, but what atheist believe to be moral usually disagrees with God's objective moral standard. You want God to stop all evil? This only works if we are using His basis of what evil is. If we are basing it off something other than God, why would He stop it? For reference, imagine you had the power to end all evil in the world. Would you end laws restricting abortion? If you are pro-life, you might have answered no. If you are pro-choice, you might have answered yes. In order to make the argument that God should stop evil, we need to go by His standard. Okay—so no sex outside of marriage, no homosexual sex, no lying of any kind, no stealing of any kind, and many other things. If you still want to be able to do these things freely (or want other people to be able to do them freely), then you are lying to yourself when you say that you want God to stop all evil. You do not want God to stop all evil. You want Him to stop your very specific view of what constitutes as evil. That simply cannot work because you are not God and you do not get to decide who God is.

The philosophical relationship we have between God and science helps me go into the next topic: evolution. I talked a little about evolution in a previous chapter. But it's important in this chapter as well. I am not an evolutionary expert, nor do I claim to be. But that isn't necessary for the argument that I am about to make. I think we can all agree, experts or not, that atheists (as a rule) believe in randomized evolution.

That's fine if they want to believe that evolution was randomized. I clearly disagree, but that doesn't matter. What matters is this question: if evolution was randomized, why does it matter if we treat other human beings with respect?

"Because humans are obviously different than animals, you idiot." Yes, of course we are. But why? Because we have feelings? Animals have feelings too. Animals can feel pain and have emotions. Should we all be vegans for that reason? Obviously not, and that isn't a straw man either if the reasoning behind not killing humans is because of a feeling of emotion from that human, that same logic can, and should be applied to animals.

One argument that sounds compelling at first from an atheistic worldview is an argument from sentience. That must count as something, right? Why should we kill sentient beings? As I've illustrated earlier, they cannot combat this other than by saying, "It's obviously wrong to kill." Those people are almost always pro-choice, which is rather ironic, is it not? If it's wrong to kill, why is it okay to kill some people and not others? Now, that's where the sentient argument comes in.

If atheists believe that human beings are valuable because of their sentience, and not some godly figure, then that is an extremely slippery slope. If being able to perceive the outside world (at least, better than any other species) is what gives us value, then killing people in their sleep, or those in a coma, should not be punished. Or at the very least, it isn't objectively bad or immoral (from the sentience argument). They will say that is a straw man too, of course. The only issue is—it's not. If the argument for not killing humans is sentience, then we should be able to kill, rape, and do basically whatever else we want with those who are not sentient. If you think this sounds absurd, you would be correct. But you simply cannot have it both ways. If things are valuable because of their feelings, emotions, or sentience, you have to draw the same line everywhere.

So either we should all be vegans, we should be able to kill people in their sleep without consequence, or God exists. Clearly the most plausible is that God exists. If the subjective reasoning that we should not harm humans is anything other than God, then you draw a false line for someone who is still alive. Either that, or we shouldn't kill or eat animals at all. For this reason, subjective morality doesn't even work.

How does this relate to God? Well, like I've said a couple of times before, without objective morality, killing humans is not always immoral. The argument against it would be "Morality is subjective." Even if that were true (which I have proved it isn't), it wouldn't matter. Going back to Hitler, if what he did was merely subjective by my own moral standard, who cares? I thought it was wrong, but he

didn't. Why does my subjective morality (if I had subjective morality) trump his subjective morality (if he had subjective morality)?
Hitler should be able to kill as many people as he so chooses without
repercussions, no? If what Hitler did was merely subjectively wrong,
and not objectively wrong, then what he did was subjectively right. I
certainly would not go down the path of saying that what Hitler did
was subjectively correct, but you have to say that if you are an atheist.
The other reality would be that objective wrongdoings exist, which
as I've illustrated, only make sense with the existence of an all-knowing being that knows what is wrong and what is right (God).

If you believe that someone should be punished for committing atrocities like Hitler did, then you and I are in the same camp,
my friend. Laws aside, our reasonings are much different if you are
saying that he should be punished because of your own subjective
standard. He obviously thought that the Jews should have been punished for whatever reason. Why does your subjective morality trump
his subjective morality? Should you be punished for doing something you believe to be morally good (let's say, giving to charity) if
someone else believes it to be subjectively immoral? Ridiculous? Yes.
Straw man? No. If you believe Hitler should have been punished for
violating your own subjective view of morality, then you could be
punished for violating someone else's subjective morality. You can't
have it both ways.

Before I go on, I need to make something clear. You do not
have to have an ultimate side of things in order to make any sort
of comparison. That is *not* what I am arguing. You can be someone
who thinks that tacos taste better than cheeseburgers for example.
We don't need a food that objectively tastes the best for us to compare it to.

But the difference in morality is that we get angry and even
punish people who have a different sense of morality than us. If
morality is subjective and an all-good being (God) is unnecessary,
then there are a couple of things worth noting:

I.   We should not get angry at someone for having a dif-
          ferent morality than us. After all, if morality is sub-

jective, and therefore comparable to taste, we cannot get rationally angry at someone for liking foods that we personally find repugnant.

II.   Going along this line, we cannot punish others for having a different subjective morality than us. Why should southern slave owners have been punished for legally owning slaves? Legality aside, what justification would one have to punish a murderer who believes he is doing a service for the community?

Keep in mind, for the time being I am not actually arguing for the existence of God. Rather, I am saying that if God does not exist and morality is subjective, we should not punish people for having a different sense of morality. Again, I bring up the subjective taste argument.

So there are only a couple of possibilities. The first possibility is that morality is subjective. Therefore, what Hitler did was only subjectively evil. If it was only subjectively evil, then it was subjectively good. If it was subjectively good, then he should not have been punished. He was merely doing what he thought was moral. Subjective moralities should not trump other subjective moralities, so he shouldn't be punished in this scenario. Again, if you still believe that Hitler should have been punished, why does your subjective morality trump his subjective morality? What makes your version of morality so special? It's only your opinion, after all.

Therefore, if Hitler should have been punished, God needs to exist. If there is an objective moral standard, God must exist. Certainly, the moral standard would be a being that knows everything. Furthermore, if morality is subjective, then Hitler should not have been punished because my subjective moral opinion cannot trump his subjective moral opinion with any continuity. If you believe Hitler's subjective morality should have been punished because he violated your subjective morality, then someone people should be punished when this happens all the time. Some people believe giving to the poor is immoral. Should you be punished for giving to the poor? If you say no, then Hitler should not have been punished. "There is a clear difference between killing people and giving money to the poor." Yes, but if it's only by your subjective standard, then it doesn't matter. I'm sure the Nazis would have said that killing Jewish people is much more moral than giving money to some homeless guy. Maybe they think that you should be punished for giving to the poor. False equivalency? Yes and no. If what Hitler did was objectively immoral, then this argument I just put forth is a major straw man. But if it isn't, and it was only subjectively immoral by your standard, it should not have been punished. Likewise, you should not be punished for doing things that you believe to be subjectively ethical. Thus, the most logical reality is that God exists, and that Hitler should be punished because he violated the objective moral law that comes from God.

It is not as if whatever God says is moral or that God says it because it is moral. Rather, God is goodness itself. As the old saying goes, "God is good all the time, and all the time, God is good." But how do we know this to be true? Well, if God exists and He created the Universe, He would have to be all-powerful. Only an all-powerful being would be able to create something from nothing. If He existed before time, He would also have to be all-present. Given that both of these realities are true, God must also be all-knowing. If God exists outside of time, He knows everything that has happened, is happening, and will happen inside of time.

Therefore, if God lacks nothing, He must be all-good. Evil is merely a lack in something good. For instance, cancer cells lack the ability to multiply correctly, Hitler lacked compassion, and so on. The idea that evil is not merely an opposition to good, but a lack in so, becomes more evident the more examples one theorizes. If God lacks *nothing*, He must be all-good. God is the standard of goodness itself.

I am not saying that theists are more moral than atheists. I have yet to see consistent scientific backing for that. Most intelligent theists do not argue with this logic. An atheist can certainly be moral. The difference is that they cannot justify that morality. If you were to ask an atheist why rape is bad, for instance, they would most likely answer with "It is immoral to violate a person's liberty." Why is this immoral? In my experience, atheists will attempt to justify their morality but will fail on account of the inevitable circular reasoning. "Murder is bad because it is bad to murder" is not an appropriate defense of your morality. For that reason, theists are able to justify morality whereas atheists cannot.

This pretty well ties into my next point, which are rights and privileges. In the United States, we have the right to peacefully assemble, keep and bear arms, speak freely (with exceptions of incitement to violence). We have been told for years that these rights were given to us by the government through the Bill of Rights.

But how can rights be given to us? After all, if the government "gives" us the right to do something, it did not exist before. Therefore, it is not a right. Now this is not an argument that we should abolish the Bill of Rights, by any means. I am merely saying that these rights do not exist without the existence of God.

Sounds asinine? Well, think of it this way: everyone agrees that rights and privileges exist. Where do these rights come from? Rights cannot be "granted" by the government. The Bill of Rights does not give us rights; it protects the rights given to us by our Creator.

To better illustrate my point, take this example: the US government passes a new amendment making rape legal. Not only do they make it legal, but it is a right for everyone to have intercourse with whomever he seems fit. Does this right exist? The government gave it to us. Therefore, there are no issues with rape after this point. Is rape only immoral before this law is passed or at all times? Obviously, just because rape is legal doesn't make it moral. Legality doesn't define morality. Just ask the slaves who were legally owned. But that isn't to say that every sin should be illegal. I don't think that people should be jailed or fined for not attending Mass. God will punish them. There's a completely different subset of laws that consist of doing something immoral to another human being against his or her will. Those are the laws that must be illegal. Our laws must coincide with God's moral standard. Just because the government says it is moral does not make it so. Consider the rape amendment and slavery as prime examples.

So the right to rape does not exist even if the government says it's okay. This analogy can be applied to just about everything. You do not have the right to steal someone's labor or get an abortion because the government says that it is morally okay. We cannot have the government be the standard of good. That has not worked out—like, ever. So if the government cannot "provide" rights, where do they come from?

A right cannot be a right if it is subjective. If I think I have the right to any shoe I want, for example, the person selling the shoes has to agree with me for the transaction to even work. Either that or there is an objective standard that tells us what rights are that the seller is obliged to follow (even if he or she disagrees).

Also, rights do not exist if they have to be given to us by the government. Like I stated earlier, you do not have a right to rape whomever you want even if it's legal. Moreover, it is not morally correct just because the government says it's okay. Therefore, these inalienable rights come from a source outside of ourselves. Everyone knows this to be God.

I don't think this is a very argumentative way of reasoning when discussing the existence of God. The reason I bring it up is to show that if these rights exist, they do not come from government. Rather, they come from an outside force.

You can call this being whatever you want: Zeus, Apollo, Allah, Yahweh, God. They are all essentially the same thing (although I'm not too sure on the specifics of Zeus and Apollo). Nevertheless, we can prove that an all-knowing, all-good, all-present being exists. A rose by any other name is still a rose. God by any other name is still God. So to say, "You believe in God but not Zeus. Why is that?" doesn't make any sense. If you want to call this omni being Zeus, go right ahead. If you want to call Him Yahweh, that's fine too although this argument from atheists makes little sense because Zeus and Apollo were created. God was not. So if Zeus and Apollo existed, they would have been created by God. Why worship the being that was created by another being? Why not worship the first being? Therefore, even if Zeus existed, there is no reason to worship him.

Even if someone believes morality is objective and does not believe in God, it is much easier to argue for universal maxims with an objective being. With that being said, this is a rational reason to believe that God exists and dictates moral standards.

Concluding Thoughts

There aren't many arguments that I view as extremely poor from either side. Each side has a specific reason for believing (or failing to believe). But of course, inadequate persuasion exists for every philosophy ever. I wanted to address these lines of reasoning before getting to more alluring ones to show atheists that I do not believe all Christian arguments to be compelling. But mostly, I want to show upcoming Christian apologetics which arguments to avoid and why we should avoid those arguments.

The first bad argument is Pascal's wager. This philosophy suggests that atheists should act as if God exists because they have nothing to lose if they do so. If Christians are wrong, they have nothing to lose. If atheists are wrong, they have everything to lose. However, this argument fails because if God doesn't exist, there is no reason to pretend of His existence. Thus, it isn't even really an argument. He is real or He is not. If He is real, He is. If not, He is not. If He is real, then we should act as if He is. If He is not, there is no rationale for pretending of His existence because He is not real. We first need to prove His existence if we are going to persuade others to act as if He is real. Simply telling atheists to pretend of His existence because they could be wrong is not conducive to a great argument. We as Christians need a better argument (and a better reason to believe) than pretending of God's existence until our inevitable death.

The next poor argument I want to address would be one of the personal experiences. Personal experiences, in their reality, are difficult to prove from a factual standpoint. Personal experiences cannot possibly be argued in a conducive way. If I told someone that I saw God or that God spoke to me, there is no way to prove that. I don't mean to demean any personal experiences people may have had with God, but those experiences are not indicative of an argument. These experiences cannot be proven incorrect by atheists but also cannot be proven correct by theists. Personal experiences, for the most part, could be considered anecdotal.

With that being said, the purpose of this book is not starting with the assumption that God exists then forcing atheists to disprove that claim. That would be like saying, "Unicorns exist. You need to disprove them." When the person who does not believe in unicorns is unable to prove that they do not exist, it would be ridiculous to then make the conclusion that unicorns exist. The same thought process can be applied with God. We should not start with the conclusion that God exists. Rather, we should start with a different hypothesis. These should be either

i.   God may or may not exist, and
ii. God does not exist.

To me, this seems like the most plausible way to talk to atheists. As a general rule, it will not convince them to come to Jesus because they cannot prove that He wasn't God. But they may come (outside of some extreme confirmation bias) if we are either able to prove that God exists or that Jesus is/was God. Proving the latter would also prove the former. Much like the unicorn example up above, one not being able to prove the existence of unicorns does not mean they exist. Likewise, someone not being able to disprove the existence of God does not mean He exists. "We live by faith, not by sight" is a common defense I have heard against this atheistic opposition from Christians. That is a satisfactory reason for belief, as far as it goes. If you want to believe in God because of a feeling and not something able to be observed, so be it. But don't expect an atheist to become Christian after that argument.

Think about this reasoning from the atheist's perspective. Would you believe in a flying spaghetti monster simply because someone told you to "Live by Faith and not by sight"? While this is a decent rule of thumb for other Christians, it is terribly persuasive for atheists. I would advise you not to use this; rather, use the arguments laid out in this book.

Notes

1   Schladebeck, J. (2019, July 06), "Late American Archbishop Fulton J. Sheen one step closer to sainthood after Pope Francis recognizes miracle," September 21, 2020, https://www.nydailynews.com/news/world/ny-archbishop-fulton-sheen-pope-francis-miracle-sainthood-20190706-pxaxldjapvfkjdeczepk2p7ula-story.html.

2   Kenneth Anderson Kitchen, *On the reliability of the Old Testament* (Wm. B. Eerdmans Publishing, 2006).

3   J. V. Kinnier-Wilson, in 11 W. Thomas, ed., Documents from Old Testament Times (London: Nelson, 1958), 14; W. G. Lambert, ITS, n.3, 16 (1965): 287–300, esp. 289, 291, 293–99, and in ISIP, 96–113, with addenda; A. R. Millard, TynB 18 (1967): 3–4, 7, 16–18, and in ISIF, 114–28; T. Iacobsen, in IBL 100 (1981): 513–29 and translation, both now in ISIF, 129–42, plus 160–66.

4   2 Peter 3:5–6.

5   Brooks, D. (2020, May 17), "Is the Black Sea Flood Noah's Great Flood?" Retrieved September 17, 2020, from https://www.historicmysteries.com/black-sea-flood/.

6   On the vast losses of ancient papyri in Egypt across the millennia see G. Posener, *College de France (Chaire de Philologie et archéologie égyptiennes), Legon inaugurale, 6 Décembre 1961* (Paris, 1962), esp. 7–12 (documents), 13–16 (sites), also (abridged) in *Annales (Economies, Sociétés, Civilisations)* 17, no. 4 (1962): 631–46.

7   Kenneth Anderson Kitchen, *On the reliability of the Old Testament* (Wm. B. Eerdmans Publishing, 2006).

8   Staedter, T. (2017, June 08), "Surprising Find: Ancient Mummy DNA Sequenced in First," retrieved September 19, 2020, from https://www.livescience.com/59410-ancient-egyptian-mummy-dna-sequenced.html.

9   Brian Kelly, "How Did the Apostles Die?" Catholicism.org, September 23, 2019.

10   1 Corinthians 15:17.

11   Dr. Simon Gathercole, "What Is the Historical Evidence That Jesus Christ Lived and Died?" *The Guardian*, April 14, 2017, Guardian News and Media.

12   Margaritoff, M. (2020, April 03), "After Millennia of Searching, Archaeologists Believe They Have Located Alexander the Great's Tomb," Retrieved June 07, 2020, from https://allthatsinteresting.com/alexander-the-great-tomb.

[13] Davis, C. Truman. "The Passion of Christ from a Medical Point of view," *Arizona medicine* (1965).

[14] Ibid.

[15] *How to Destroy Christianity With One Easy Step* [Video file]. (2015, October 18). Retrieved 2019, from https://www.youtube.com/watch?v=-JMF6hkOnmY.

[16] "Modalism," *Merriam-Webster*, accessed August 7, 2020, https://www.merriam-webster.com/dictionary/modalism.

[17] John 1:14.

[18] 1 Corinthians 6:14.

[19] 1 Corinthians 11:3.

[20] John 14:26.

[21] Acts 8:29.

[22] John 14:12

[23] John 16:7

[24] Revelation 22:1

[25] John 7:38-39

[26] Alister McGrath, *Iustitia Dei: A History of the Christian Doctrine of Justification*. Vol. I. Pg. 186 (emphasis mine)

[27] Philip Schaff: *History of the Christian Church, volume II: Ante-nicene Christianity.* AD 100–325, Christian Classics Ethereal Library. (n.d.). Retrieved March 14, 2022, from https://ccel.org/ccel/schaff/hcc2/hcc2.v.xiv.xviii.html

[28] J.N.D. Kelly, *Early Christian Doctrines* (New York: HarperCollins, 1978), 193–194

[29] Carson, D. A., et al. *The Doctrine on Which the Church Stands or Falls (Foreword by DA Carson): Justification in Biblical, Theological, Historical, and Pastoral Perspective*. Crossway, 2019.

[30] Sproul, Robert Charles. *What is reformed Theology?: Understanding the basics*. Baker Books, 2005. Pg 84 and 90.

[31] "Trent Horn vs. Dr. James R. White—Can a Christian Lose Their Salvation? (Full Debate)." *YouTube*, 31 Jan. 2017

[32] Titus 2:11

[33] 2 Peter 3:9.

[34] Harmon, E., & Zebell, T. (2016, February 02). Did god cause the fall of man? Retrieved February 10, 2021, from https://authorofsin.pressbooks.com/chapter/did-god-cause-the-fall-of-man/#:~:text=According%20to%20Calvinism,%20Adam%E2%80%99s%20sin%20was%20in%20accordance,or%20befel,%20Adam%20was%20so%20ordained%20of%20God.%E2%80%9D

[35] Romans 8:38–39.

[36] James 2:19.

[37] Romans 1:16; Mark 16:16.

[38] Larry Peterson (October 12, 2017), "Did you know the 1st apparition of the Blessed Mother was an act of bilocation?" Aleteia, retrieved September 23, 2020.

39 ————(May 8, 2018), "England's only approved Marian apparition gives us a peek at Nazareth," Aleteia, retrieved October 10, 2019. The importance of Our Lady of Walsingham is shown through pontifical approbation (recognition), which has been given to it by four popes: Pope Leo XIII, in 1897; Pope Pius XII, in 1954; Pope St. John Paul II, in 1982; and Pope Francis, in 2015.

40 "La Madonna della Guardia: Un Culto Deciso a Tavolino" (in Italian). la Repubblica. August 29, 2010. Nel 1915 il papa genovese Benedetto XV (Giacomo Della Chiesa) dà un notevole appoggio all'affermazione del «nuovo» culto, elevando a «basilica minore» il nuovo santuario.

41 "Vailankanni, India: Basilica of Our Lady of Good Health," "The Lourdes of the East," The Catholic Traveler, retrieved October 10, 2019.

42 "Ten Things to Know About Our Lady of Guadalupe," University of Dayton, January 27, 2016, retrieved October 5, 2019. The church approved the apparition in 1555.

43 Jim Graves (March 31, 2011), "Marian Messenger," National Catholic Register, retrieved October 6, 2019.

44 "Envoy Named for Centenary of Lithuania Apparitions," Zenit, August 22, 2008, retrieved August 27, 2020.

45 Ann Ball, *The Other Faces of Mary: Stories, Devotions, and Pictures of the Holy Virgin Around the World*, (2004), 153.

46 Katherine Arcement, "Our Lady of Fatima: The Virgin Mary Promised Three Kids a Miracle That 70,000 Gathered to See," *The Washington Post*, WP Company, April 1, 2019.

47 Joe Nickell, *Looking for a miracle: weeping icons, relics, stigmata, visions & healing cures* (Prometheus Books, 2009).

48 Mark, "Debunking the Sun Miracle Skeptics," The Now Word, October 14, 2017.

49 Romans 3:28.

50 Deuteronomy 16:12–16

51 Dr. Taylor Marshall, "Did God Command Genocide in Deuteronomy?" September 28, 2015. https://taylormarshall.com/2012/01/did-god-command-genocide-in-deuteronomy.html.

52 Deuteronomy 22:28–29.

53 GotQuestions.org. "Home." GotQuestions.org, October 20, 2011. https://www.gotquestions.org/Bible-rape.html.

54 "2 Kings 2:23–24: Elisha and the Bears." New Christian Bible Study, accessed August 12, 2020. https://newchristianbiblestudy.org/bible/story/elisha-and-the-bears/king-james-version.

55 Paul Copan, *Is God a Moral Monster?: Making Sense of the Old Testament God* (Baker Books, 2011).

56 2 Timothy 3:16.

57 Genesis 17:10.

58 Romans 3:28.

[59] Hebrews 8:13.

[60] Exodus 32:14.

[61] Team, BibleAsk, and BibleAsk Team BibleAsk composes of a group of team members dedicated to answering Bible Questions! "Who Wrote the First Five Books of the Bible?" October 18, 2019, https://bibleask.org/who-wrote-the-first-five-books-of-the-bible/.

[62] GotQuestions.org. "Home." GotQuestions.org, June 10, 2014. https://www.gotquestions.org/Judah-conquered-by-Babylon.html.

[63] Ecclesiastes 1:4.

[64] Isaiah 1:14, 43:24.

[65] Isaiah 40:28.

[66] Genesis 32:30; Exodus 33:20; Genesis 12:7; Exodus 33:11; John 1:18; Exodus 24:9–1; 1 Timothy 6:16.

[67] Mark 10:46; Luke 18:35.

[68] Matthew 20:30.

[69] Mark 11:12–17.

[70] Matthew 21:12, 21:17–19.

[71] Wayne Brindle, "The Census and Quirinius: Luke 2:2" (1984). SOR Faculty Publications and Presentations. 73. https://digitalcommons.liberty.edu/sor_fac_pubs/73.

[72] Mark 15:37–38; Matthew 27:50–51.

[73] Luke 23:45–46.

[74] Luke 23:39–42.

[75] Mark 15:32; Matthew 27:44.

[76] Matthew 28:2.

[77] Luke 24:2.

[78] John 3:13.

[79] Genesis 1:25–27.

[80] Genesis 2:18–19.

[81] Deuteronomy 12:31.

[82] 2 Samuel 24:9.

[83] 1 Chronicles 21:5.

[84] "2 Samuel 24:9-Why Do the Numbers of Men Recorded in 2 Samuel 24:9 and in 1 Chronicles 21:5–6 Disagree?" Defending Inerrancy, January 1, 2015. https://defendinginerrancy.com/bible-solutions/2_Samuel_24.9.php.

[85] Newton: "A Quote from the Principia." *Goodreads*, Goodreads, https://www.goodreads.com/quotes/232391-this-most-beautiful-system-of-the-sun-planets-and-comets.

[86] Darwin: "Charles Darwin Quote." *Lib Quotes*, https://libquotes.com/charles-darwin/quote/lbz0r6s.

[87] Braun: Bergman, Jerry. "Wernher Von Braun: The Father of Space Flight." *The Institute for Creation Research*

88 Charles R. Marshall, "Explaining the Cambrian 'explosion' of animals," *Annu. Rev. Earth Planet. Sci.* 34 (2006): 355–384.

89 Georges Lemaitre: Father of the Big Bang: AMNH (*Home* nd). Retrieved January 20, 2021, from https://www.amnh.org/learn-teach/curriculum-collections/cosmic-horizons-book/georges-lemaitre-big-bang#:~:text=Georges%20Lema%C3%AEtre,%20(1894-1966),%20Belgian%20cosmologist,%20Catholic%20priest,%20and,Georges%20Lema%C3%AEtre,%20a%20Belgian%20cosmologist%20and%20Catholic%20priest.

90 Fred Hoyle and Nalin Chandra Wickramasinghe, *Evolution from space* (JM Dent, 1981).

91 Nola Taylor Redd, "How Old Is the Universe?" June 8, 2017. https://www.space.com/24054-how-old-is-the-universe.html.

92 "Fine-Tuning for Life on Earth." Reasons to Believe, accessed August 20, 2020. https://reasons.org/explore/blogs/todays-new-reason-to-believe/read/tnrtb/2004/06/07/fine-tuning-for-life-on-earth-updated-june-2004.

About the Author

Parker Manning is a Catholic apologist who wants others to learn about the one true faith through his writing. Parker is currently studying to be an economics professor. This is his second piece of writing, his first one is called "Fundamentals of Catholic Theology in Just Over 100 Pages". That book focuses more on the specifics of Catholic and Protestant theology rather than the existence of God as a whole